GARDEN TERMS

MICHAEL PILCHER, LISA DAVIES AND
DAVID HURRION

HAMLYN

First published in 1995
by Hamlyn
an imprint of Reed Consumer Books Limited
Michelin House, 81 Fulham Road, London SW3 6RB
and Auckland, Melbourne, Singapore and Toronto
in conjunction with Amateur Gardening,
IPC Magazines Limited
Westover House, West Quay Road, Poole,
Dorset BH15 1JG

ISBN 0 600 58428 3

Printed in Finland

A catalogue record for this book is available
from the British Library

GARDEN TERMS

CONTENTS

INTRODUCTION

There was a time when gardening was wrapped up in all manner of myth and mystery. There were secret formulations for feeds and fertilizers, specific ways of doing things that were the secret of the head gardener and so many technical terms that potential gardeners were discouraged from becoming involved because gardening seemed like another language.

Times have changed, and the late Percy Thrower probably did much to bring gardening to the masses, to such an extent that it is now one of our most popular and ever-growing hobbies.

The *Amateur Gardening Garden Terms* has been written with this philosophy in mind. All three authors spent many hours during their horticultural training getting to grips with a varied (and often confusing) horticultural vocabulary which meant little to the wider world.

It is often assumed, and quite wrongly, that gardeners all have the same level of knowledge and understanding of the subject. By explaining concisely what particular words mean, or relate to, *Garden Terms* should make a browse through any magazine or book, a visit to a garden centre or viewing any gardening programme on television more of a pleasure and less of a headache!

8

Metric/Imperial Conversions

LENGTH

Imperial	Metric
1 inch	25.4mm
1 foot	305mm
1 yard	0.914 metre
1 mile	1.609km

Metric	Imperial
1mm	0.039in
10mm (1cm)	0.394in
1 metre	1.094yd
1km	0.6214 mile

Approximate guide:
4in = 100mm   11yd = 10 metres
6 miles = 10 kilometres

WEIGHT

Imperial	Metric
1 lb	0.4536kg
1 ton	1.0161 tonnes

Metric	Imperial
1 kg (1000kg)	2.2046lb
1 tonne (1000kg)	0.9842 ton

CAPACITY

Imperial	Metric
1 cu yd	0.7646cm³

Metric	Imperial
1m³	1.308yd³

Approximate guide: 4yd³ = 3mm³

CONVERSION FACTORS

To convert to metric, multiply by the factor shown. To convert from metric divide by the factor.

Length
Miles: kilometres	1.6093
Yards: metres	0.9144
Feet: metres	0.3048
Inches: millimetres	25.4
Inches: centimetres	2.54

Area
Square miles: square kilometres	2.59
Square miles: hectares	258.999
Acres: square metres	4046.86
Acres: hectares	0.4047
Square yards: square metres	0.8361
Square feet: square metres	0.0929
Square feets: square centimetres	929.03
Square inches: square millimetres	645.16
Square inches: square centimetres	6.4516

AREA

Imperial	Metric
1sq ft (ft²)	0.093m²
1 sq yd (yd²)	0.836m²
1 acre (4840yd²)	4046.86m²

Metric	Imperial
1m²	10.76ft²
1m²	1.196yd²
1 hectare (10,000m²)	2.4711 acres

Approximate guide: 12yd² = 10m²

TEMPERATURES

°F	°C	°F	°C
5	-15	-15	5
10	-12.2	-12	10.4
15	-9.4	-9	15.8
20	-6.7	-6	21.2
25	-3.9	-3	26.6
30	-1.1	0	32
35	1.7	3	37.4
40	4.4	6	42.8
45	7.2	9	48.2
50	10	12	53.6
55	12.8	15	59
60	15.6	18	64.4
65	18.3	21	69.8
70	21.1	24	75.2
75	23.9	27	80.6
80	26.7	30	86
85	29.4	33	91.4
90	32.2	36	96.8
95	35	39	102.2
100	37.8	42	107.6
105	40.6	45	113
110	43.3	48	118.4
115	46.1	51	123.8
120	48.9	54	129.2
125	51.7	57	134.6
130	54.4	60	140
135	57.2		
140	60		

VOLUME

Cubic yards: cubic metres	0.7646
Cubic feet: cubic metres	0.0283
Cubic feet: cubic decimetres	28.3168
Cubic inches: cubic centimetres	16.3871

Capacity

Gallons: litres	4.546
Pints: litres	0.568

Mass

Tons: kilograms	1016.05
Tons: tonnes	1.0160
Hundredweights: kilograms	50.8023
Stones: kilograms	6.3503
Pounds: kilograms	0.4536
Ounces: grams	28.3495

Mass per unit area
Pounds per square foot:

kilograms per square metre	4.8824

Pounds per square inch:

grams per square centimetre	70.307

Ounces per square foot:

grams per square metre	305.152

A-Z DIRECTORY

A QUICK REFERENCE GUIDE TO
EVERY GARDEN TERM

A

Abaxial Underside of a leaf, facing away from the stem; it is normally ridged with protruding veins. In most leaves, this side of the leaf bears the majority of the stomata through which the gaseous exchange will take place.

Abscissic acid Chemical hormone contained in plant cells which triggers leaf abscission.

Abscission The process of leaf fall caused by the formation of a layer of impermeable cells between the stem and the leaf. It is triggered by the production of chemical hormones. *N.B. Absciss layer*

Acaricide Natural or man-made chemical which is used as a pesticide to kill mites.

Acclimatization Process by which environmental factors, such as temperature, moisture and light, are gradually changed to acclimatize plants to new growing conditions. Without this, plants may suffer damage in the new environment in which they are placed.

Achene A one-seeded, dry fruit, formed from one carpel in the flower.

Acicular Having the shape of a needle and normally applied to the form of leaves.

Acid Term used to describe soils with a pH of less than 7. Acid soils are deficient in lime, but most plants will grow on them. Ericaceous plants need acidic soil to thrive. The pH of a soil can be raised by the application of lime.

Acre Imperial measurement of land area equivalent to 43560sq ft (4047sq m) [Scottish acre 55354sq ft (5143sq m); Irish acre 70560sq ft (6555sq m)].

Actinomorphic Flowers which are symmetrical in all directions when viewed from above, with each whorl consisting of organs of the same size.

Active transport The uptake and movement of substances through the plant, requiring energy from stored sugars. Minerals and other large molecules are moved around the plant by this process.

Acuminate Leaf tip shape in which the edges of the leaf taper to a fine point.

Acute Leaf tip where the edges taper sharply to a wide point.

Adaptation Characteristics of plants and other organisms which help them to survive and reproduce in a particular habitat. Adaptations are assimilated by the evolutionary process and natural selection in response to the conditions in which the plant is growing.

Adaxial Top side of a leaf, facing the stem, flatter than the leaf's underside and usually covered with a thick, waxy cuticle to reduce water loss by evaporation.

Adelgid Sap-sucking insect pest, closely related to aphids, which causes damage to ornamental and crop plants.

Adnate attached the whole length to another structure

Adpressed Parts of a plant or flower which are closely pressed together but not united or fused.

Adventitious Roots or shoots arising from a place where growths do not normally occur. Adventitious roots may arise from stems; adventitious shoots may develop on stems rather than from leaf axils. Such buds grow from pieces of meristematic tissue, which is left behind as the plant grows. Cells in this region divide rapidly causing the roots or shoots to develop.

Aeration Process by which air enters the soil through a network of pores. Air is necessary in the soil for healthy root growth. Also the action of loosening compacted soil to allow air to enter. Benefits include air at the plant roots and improved drainage. Tined aerators are used on turf. Digging or forking is carried out to aerate beds and borders.

Aerial root Root which arises from part of the plant above soil level to provide anchorage and to absorb moisture from the air. Aerial roots are produced mostly by plants growing in moist environment. Some climbing species produce aerial roots which are used to cling to surfaces.

Aerator Hand or powered tool used in the process of aerating turf.

Aestivation The way in which the parts of a flower are arranged in respect to each other.

Agar Nutrient gel, prepared from seaweed, on which seed can be pre-germinated. Also used in micropropagation.

Aggregate Crushed stone or gravel used in making concrete to give strength and to reduce the volume needed of more expensive constituents.

Also an accumulation of soil particles into a larger unit, such as a clod.

Agriculture Practice of cultivating the land in order to grow plants and rear animals for food.

Agrostology The study of grasses, botany, morphology and nomenclature.

Air frost Occurs when the temperature of the air falls below freezing. Cold air is unable to hold much moisture and therefore droplets of water may be deposited onto a surface where they form crystals of ice. Air frost may damage leafy growths and unripened flowers. Soft, water-filled shoots and leaves may be blackened by the action of frost which freezes the water in the cells, which when defrosted then expands, rupturing the cell walls.

Air layering Plant propagation process whereby adventitious roots are encouraged to grow from a stem. The process involves wrapping a prepared stem with sphagnum moss and enclosing the whole with polythene to encourage root formation. It is used on stems which are too high to bring down to ground level for conventional layering. Once roots have been produced, the plantlet can be detached and potted up to grow on as an individual.

Air temperature Refers to the heat produced by the radiant energy received from the sun (solar radiation). The radiation is mostly received at short wavelengths which heats the air and surface of the earth. The stored energy at ground level is re-radiated back into the air which may prevent the air from cooling. Air heats up and cools down more quickly than soil or plant tissue and so the air (ambient) temperature can fluctuate greatly between day (when heat in the form of solar radiation is being received) and night (when energy is being lost into the upper atmosphere). Air temperature decreases by 0.5°C (-33°F) with every 300m (1000ft) increase in altitude.

Algae Large group of predominantly aquatic plants. Some algae are able to grow on paving which can cause it to become slippery.

Algicide Chemical which kills algae.

Alkaline This term is used to describe soils that have a pH that is greater than 7. Most plants, except ericaceous subjects, will grow quite successfully on soil which is slightly alkaline. Some reduction of alkalinity can be afforded by the application of peat, or similar non-alkaline organic matter, and flowers of sulphur. However, this is only realistic with soils that are marginally alkaline.

Alkaloid Many plants produce these organic compounds which contain nitrogen. The majority are toxic and protect the plant from being eaten.

Alpine Plant which has adapted to growing above the tree line in mountain regions of the world. Most alpine species are diminutive and produce flowers early in the season.

Alpine house Unheated glasshouse used for growing and displaying moisture sensitive alpine plants.

Allelopathy Inhibition, by a particular plant, of the growth of surrounding plants by toxins.

Alloxydim-sodium Foliage-absorbed chemical used as a selective weedkiller on most perennial grasses. Useful for controlling couch grass in flower beds and rock gardens.

Alluvial soil Soil formed from alluvium, which is a river-borne material. Alluvial soils are generally very fertile.

Alternate Arrangement of single leaves in succession along a shoot or branch, each leaf positioned at a different position around the stem.

Alternate host Plant on which a pest or disease exists for part of its life cycle and from which it can infect another plant.

Alternation of generations Life cycle which involves two different forms of a plant, one form developing asexually, the other sexually. It is necessary for the plant to go through both stages in order to reach maturity.

Altitude The height or elevation of a point, measured above sea level. Given the same latitude, sites which are at a high altitude are colder than those at lower levels. For each 300m (1000ft) increase in altitude, the temperature of the air drops by 0.5°C (-33°F).

Aluminium ammonium sulphate This term refers to a bitter tasting metallic salt which is used as an ingredient in bird and animal repellents.

Aluminium sulphate Metallic salt. Active chemical ingredient of slug- and snail-killers.

Ambient temperature The temperature of the air that is affected by the radiant energy received from the sun, which is known as solar radiation.

Amelioration Term used to describe the action of improving a soil by the addition of organic matter, coarse grit for drainage, fertilizers or any process of cultivation, in order to make the growing conditions better for plant roots.

Amitrole This is a foliage-acting, trans-located chemical which is widely used as a weedkiller.

Ammonia Inorganic chemical molecule composed of nitrogen and hydrogen, released by the decomposition of organic manures. Ammonia is toxic to plants, although it contains nitrogen which is essential for leafy growth, and it needs to be broken down by denitrifying bacteria which release the nitrates which can then be used by the plant.

Ammonium nitrate Chemical, inorganic fertilizer containing a high percentage of nitrogen in the form of nitrate which can be used by plants to give growth to both leaves and shoots.

Ammonium sulphamate Foliage- and soil-acting chemical used for the control of woody-stemmed perennial weeds.

Anatomy The arrangement of tissues and organs to form a plant (or animal).

Androecium This is the collective name for the male, pollen-producing parts of a flower consisting of the stamens. Each stamen is composed of an anther, which bears the pollen, and a filament which supports the anther.

Anemophily Pollination which occurs by means of the wind. Plants which are anemophilous often produce flowers in a pendulous or erect catkin, usually without petals, scent or nectar, and produce vast quantities of pollen. The anthers of such flowers often hang outside to release pollen into the wind.

Angiosperm One of the main divisions of flowering plants in which the seeds are carried in a closed ovary or seed case.

Annual Plant which completes its life cycle (from germination, through flowering to seed production) and dies in a single growing season. Hardy annuals are generally sown directly into the ground where they are to flower and are able to

survive frost. They may be sown in the spring, or even in the preceding autumn to flower in the summer. Half-hardy annuals are able to withstand cool conditions but not frost; these plants are generally sown under glass and planted in their flowering positions when the risk of frost has passed.

Annual border Bed which is planted up with a temporary, seasonal display of annual, biennial or even perennial plants.

Annual ring Ring of tissue in woody stems, formed from cells produced by the cambium, which denote the amount of growth in girth of the stem in a particular season. Rapid growth in spring is seen as a lighter coloured region; slower growth in the summer results in darker coloration and together this gives the impression of concentric rings when a slice is taken through a woody stem. The rings can be counted in old trees to gauge the age of the plant.

Anthesis The opening of the flower bud and the expansion of the various organs of the flower to allow cross-pollination.

Anther The part of the stamen or androecium which produces pollen. This structure is lobed and hollow, containing masses of pollen grains which are released when the anther splits or dehisces. The anther is borne on a stalk or filament.

Anthracnose Plant disease caused by a fungus and characterized by dark sunken stripes or spots.

Ants Insect whose colonies may cause problems in loosening the soil around plants and sometimes burying alpine subjects or grass. Ants harvest honeydew from aphids and may be seen climbing stems, but they do no direct damage to the plants.

Apetalous Flowers which do not bear petals. Often wind pollinated, they do not need to attract insects and the stamens and stigma usually protrude from the flower.

Apex The extreme tip of a stem or root tip where growth potential is at its greatest. Cell division occurs immediately behind this region. Also used to refer to the tip of a leaf.

Aphid This is a plant sap–sucking insect that feeds by means of a stylet which is inserted into the plant tissues. Aphids exude sticky honeydew and may transfer diseases from one plant to another as they move about to feed.

Aphicide Chemical which is mainly active in killing aphids. Aphicides may kill on contact or have a systemic action, in which the chemical is taken up into the tissues of the plant and transferred into the aphid when it feeds.

Apical bud The large bud at the end of a shoot, stem or branch.

Apical dominance Condition where the main bud at the tip of a shoot grows while the side buds are suppressed. Inhibition of the side buds is caused by chemicals which are produced in the shoot tip. Removal of the tip allows side shoots to develop.

Apical meristem This term describes the region near the tip of the stem or root where cells are capable of rapid division which results in extension growth.

Apiculate With a little point

Apomictic Plant capable of producing propagules or potential new individuals from the female reproductive organs without the need for fertilization. The resulting individuals are usually genetically identical, although mutations can occur to produce variations in the new plants.

Aquatic Plant that grows in water. They may be rooted with emergent or floating leaves, totally submerged or free-floating.

Arborescent Branched or growing in the form of a tree.

Arboretum Area of land devoted to growing a living collection of tree species in conditions which allow them to display their forms and characteristics for comparison and identification.

Arboriculture The practice of tree and shrub culture, including propagation, planting, pruning, felling and the nomenclature of trees and shrubs.

Arbour Small recess enclosed by the foliage of trees, shrubs or climbing plants; it may incorporate a seat.

Arch Structure of wood, metal, stone or brick, built to support climbing plants over a pathway or seat.

Architectural plant Plant which bears large, boldly shaped leaves or which has a distinctive stem structure or form. Architectural plants make a dramatic contrast to small-leaved plants and may be grown as specimens to create a focal point.

Areole Modified side shoot on cactus which takes the form of a small swelling surmounted by small hairs and spines.

Arid Used to refer to a climate which is characterized by very low rainfall and which supports desert or semi-desert vegetation. Such plants have evolved to cope with drought conditions by possessing far-reaching roots, succulent stems and waxy coatings which help to reduce water loss.

Aril Fleshy outer seed covering in addition to the seed coat. Often coloured; ie red berry-like structure seen on yew.
common in Euphorbia family)

Aristate Bearing bristles, usually on seed-head or flower.

Armed Bearing thorns or spines on stems or leaves. These structures give the plant protection from grazing by animals.

Aroid Plant belonging to the *Araceae* family, often producing aerial roots which absorb moisture from the atmosphere.

Arris rail Length of timber, mounted horizontally between two posts used to support thin, vertical strips of wood or featherboard, to make a fence structure. At least two arris rails are required to support the boarding and they are generally triangular in cross section which allows them to be strong but at the same time limits their weight and expense.

Asexual reproduction Form of reproduction which does not involve the mixing of genetic information via male and female gametes. Includes apomictic plants and the production of plantlets.

Ash Remains of a wood fire that can be used as a plant fertilizer, since it contains useful amounts of phosphate and potash which encourage healthy root growth and flower production.

Aspect Direction in which a particular object faces to receive optimum amount of light. In the northern hemisphere places with a southerly aspect generally receive the most direct sunlight; those with a northerly aspect receive the least.

Asphalt Bituminous substance, obtained as a residue from the distillation of petrol. Used as a surfacing material, usually with stone chippings rolled into the surface to make it harder wearing and also as a waterproofing layer on some roofs.

Astringent **Contracting or binding**

Attenuate Shape formed by a leaf blade tapering in hollow curves to the leaf petiole or stalk.

Atomize The process of reducing a liquid to a fine spray or mist for application to plants. Liquids in this form are liable to drift in currents of air and may affect plants or animals nearby.

Auger Instrument comprising a large, coarse-grade thread on a handle, used for taking cores from the soil for testing. Smaller bore augers are used for extracting samples from the trunks of trees to check for decay.

Auricle Ear-shaped structure found at the base of the leaf of particular grasses. The shape and size of these structures can be used as a means of identifying and naming grasses.

Autogamy Self-fertilization in which pollen from the stamens pollinates and fertilizes the same flower. Pollen may simply drop onto the style or be transferred by wind or insects. Such flowers have developed this ability to increase their potential to produce seed even if not cross-pollinated from other flowers.

Autotrophic Ability of most plants to synthesize their own food from simple chemicals using the energy from light or chemical reactions. This makes plants the primary producers in food chains, with herbivorous animals feeding on them to gain their nutrition.

Auxin Growth-controlling hormone regulating stem and root growth as well as other plant processes.

Avenue Refers to a walk or drive that is lined with parallel rows of trees or shrubs and used originally to create a grand entrance to large country estates. Avenues are used in formal gardens to create perspective and also in towns and cities to bring greenery to thoroughfares.

Awl-shaped Tapering to a narrow and stiff point.

Awn Bristle or sharp point attached to the seed of some grasses which gives the seedhead a brush-like appearance.

Axil The internal angle formed between a leaf or its petiole, and the stem of a plant.

Axillary bud Also known as a side bud, these buds are formed in the axil between the leaf petiole and the main stem. Such buds are often inhibited from growing by the apical bud, which is carried at the tip of the stem.

Axis Term which is used to describe a stem or central organ from which other organs grow.

B

Back-bulb The leafless pseudobulb of an orchid used for food storage. Pseudobulbs provide the energy for the production of new bulbs, leaves and flowers.

Backfill The process of filling a planting hole around the roots of a plant. Backfilling should be carried out in stages, incorporating layers of soil which should be firmed thoroughly at each stage to ensure that it is in intimate contact with the roots.

Bacteria Microscopic, single-celled organisms. May be parasitic or saprophytic. Some forms of bacteria are pathogens of decorative or crop plants causing a variety of plant diseases.

Bactericide Chemical which is used to kill bacteria.

Ball Firmed soil or compost around the root system of a plant which is used to maintain moisture at the plant roots and to limit the effects of damage to the essential fine roots and root hairs during the transplanting.

The root ball can be formed by digging around the plant with a spade and levering it out of the ground. Once lifted it is then wrapped in hessian or plastic in order to retain the soil around the roots.

Bale Bundle of peat or compost in a semi-compacted form, normally wrapped in packaging for ease of transport. The material should be broken up thoroughly and moistened before use.

Balustrade Ornamental rail comprising supporting posts (balusters) and coping.

Bamboo Term used generally to describe the hollow canes that are produced from the stems of bamboo plants. These are harvested and dried for use as natural-looking plant supports.

Bank General term referring to an inclined profile of soil or plants. A bank of soil needs to rest at a low angle so that it does not slump or become eroded due to rainwater run off. Banks of plants are formed by planting tall-growing speci-mens at the back of the border to provide a framework, low-growing plants at the front and medium-sized species in the intermediate area between.

Bare-root Plants sold without soil around their roots. Some plants, especially imported specimens, may have all the soil washed from their roots to limit the spread of soil-borne pests and diseases. Bare-root plants need to be planted carefully, with the soil or compost in intimate contact with the roots so that they are kept moist and encouraged to produce fibrous feeder roots.

Bark Protective layer of tissue, usually cork and phloem, on the outside of the woody stems of trees and shrubs. New tissue produced from the actively dividing cambium layer is added to this layer each year. As new material is added, the bark on the outside has to stretch and split to accommodate the extra volume.

Bark-ringing Process of removing a ring of bark from around a stem or branch to reduce vigorous growth and to encourage the formation of fruit in some trees. Bark ringing may also be caused by grazing animals and may then have detrimental effects. Removal of phloem underneath the bark may restrict the transport of sugars down to the plant roots. If bark ringing occurs on the main trunk then, although the roots will still be able to supply the top growth with water for a short period, the lack of sugar will mean that they cannot be maintained or grow and will eventually die.

Barrow Wheeled cart with handle(s) for transporting materials over a distance. The cart may have one or more wheels.

Basal plate Compressed portion of stem forming the base of a bulb, from which the roots, leaves and stems grow. Bulbils also arise from this plate of tissue. The basal plate of any bulb needs to be in good condition if the bulb is to remain healthy and grow. Any damage to the basal plate may result in fungal infection, causing the bulb to rot.

Base dressing Quantity of fertilizer or organic matter applied to an area of soil prior to sowing or planting. The base dressing is intended to be a supply of nutrients for the first 6-8 weeks and additional fertilizer should be applied in the form of liquids or solids to maintain healthy growth.

Basic slag Refers to the waste product from the manufacture of steel containing calcium phosphate. This is used as a fertilizer for the supply of phosphate for healthy root growth and calcium for general plant health.

Basin irrigation This term describes a method of watering plants which involves creating a shallow depression around the base of plant and then filling it with water and allowing the water to soak in without running off the surface. Basins can be formed by excavating a dish in the earth over the root area or by mounding soil in a circle at a short distance from the stem of the plant. Take care not to damage any fibrous roots located just under the surface of the soil. Also avoid piling the soil close to the main stem as this could cause it to rot.

Bast phloem

Bearded Covering of long or stiff hairs on a flower or seedhead.

Bed system Method of growing crops in close blocks with peripheral access in order to limit soil compaction and ease cultivation. Bed systems are also ideal for allowing efficient crop rotation, each bed can be planted with a different crop to avoid pests and diseases being transferred to subsequent plants.

Bedding plants Plants which are temporarily planted out, prior to maturity, for the duration of their flower display. Traditionally this involves using annuals, biennials and tender perennials, but any plant may be used in this manner to bring colour and life to a border. Summer bedding plants may be grown under glass from seed or cuttings and hardened off ready for planting out in late spring; spring bedding plants can be sown in nursery rows and grown on outdoors ready to plant out in early autumn, while some species can be divided to produce new plants.

Beetle Insect which is part of the largest group of animals in the world and includes scavenging, carnivorous, plant feeding, wood-eating and water-dwelling types. A limited number of beetles are pests. The larvae of many beetles are also pests of ornamentals or vegetable crops.

Beneficial insect Any insect which acts as a predator or parasite on a plant pest, or an insect which pollinates flowers.

Benomyl This term describes an active chemical ingredient that is used as a fungicide.

Berry Entire pulpy fruit usually containing a number of seeds. Some examples of this are gooseberry, grape and currant. The pulp may contain a chemical inhibitor which prevents the seeds from germinating; once this has been broken down, the seeds can take up water.

Biennial A plant that flowers and dies during the second growing season after overwintering. Biennials are sown and germinate in their first season and make a resting bud in which to survive the winter. In the spring of the following season, top growth restarts and flowers are then produced. Many biennials are used as spring bedding plants and are sown in the late summer of one year, ready to flower in the spring of the following year.

Biennial cropping Plant which bears heavy crops of flower and fruit in alternate years with little or no crop in the intervening years. It is not really understood why some plants do this but it may be due to the fact that all available nutrients and food stores are used up in producing the abundance of flowers and fruit and the plant has to accumulate fresh reserves over the subsequent year before it can produce again.

Bifurcate Divided into two branches or stalks. This term is used to refer to parts of the stem or to leaves which are divided.

Bifoliate Having two leaves on each leaf stalk or petiole.

Big bud Condition of buds which are unusually rounded and sometimes split, due to infestation of mite pest. Such buds will not develop properly into leaves, stems and flowers. Control is difficult and while removing infected buds can be partially successful, some plants may be so overrun with the pest that the best thing is to grub up the specimens, burn them and start again with fresh plants.

Bigeneric hybrid Plant genus resulting from crossing two different genera. Such a hybrid may show some characteristics of each of the parents or it may be intermediate between the two.

Binomial classification Term given to the classification of organisms, including plants, using two Latin words. The first word denotes the genus to which the species of plant belongs eg *Malus* and the second identifies the species as distinct from other species which may be present in the same genus eg *sylvestris*. The generic name is denoted by carrying an upper case first letter; the specific name carries lower case. This system of classification was introduced by the botanist Linnaeus.

Adaptations to the basic system include the further sub-division of the species into subspecies, varieties and hybrids.

Biological control Non-chemical system of limiting pest and disease populations with parasitic or predatory organisms. Such organisms reach peak populations a short while after the peak of the pest and so there may be a short time lapse before heavy infestations are brought under control. This natural system of pest- and disease-control does without the need for chemicals but the predators may need to be reintroduced in subsequent years as they rarely survive in sufficient numbers to afford effective control.

Biology The study of living organisms. Also used to refer to the living organisms of a particular area.

Bipinnate Leaf that is divided into several sections which are again sub-divided.

Bitter pit Disorder of apples, thought to be physiological in origin, where the flesh of fruit is marked with brown spots.

Bitumen Residual substance remaining after the distillation of oil which is used as a surfacing material for paths and also as a waterproofing for flat roofs. Bitumen may have gravel or stone chippings rolled into the surface to provide better wear on paths.

Blackfly Common name referring to a form of aphid which is a pest of a number of plant species. It feeds by means of a pointed stylet or mouthpart which is pushed into the plant tissues and through which it sucks sap. These pests may have an effect on the general health of the infested plant .

Black leg Disease caused by one or more fungi and bacteria which destroys pelargonium cuttings and sometimes bedded-out plants.

Blade Term that describes the flattened structure of the leaf formed by the thin layers of cells between the veins. Cells in the leaf blade contain chlorophyll which is responsible for photosynthesis and the production of sugar which the plant uses to function and grow.

Blanching Process by which light is excluded from leaves or stems in order to keep them tender and prevent the development of green coloration in the tissue. Light may be excluded by wrapping stems with cardboard, by using proprietary plant collars, by mounding soil around the base of the plant or by covering the whole plant with a flowerpot.

Bleeding Exudation of plant sap from the cut end of a stem, leaf or root. Plants continue to exude sap until a callus is formed which will seal the wound.

Blight Common name given to a pest or disease which causes withering in plant tissues without rotting.

Blind Failure to flower in a plant or stem. Blindness may be due to infestation by a pest or disease or as a result of incorrect growing conditions in the previous season.

Blood, fish and bone General plant fertilizer which is made from ground fish and waste products from the meat industry. It provides nitrogen and phosphorous to encourage leaf and root growth.

Bloom A flower or blossom. Also used to describe the fine, white or bluish waxy coating on stems, leaves or fruit.

Blossom Term used to describe the flower(s) or flowering of a plant, particularly of edible fruit species. Flowers may be held singly in a blossom or mass together to form an inflorescence.

Blown State of flowers or headed vegetables which are past their best, where the petals or leaves have become loose and discoloured. Flowers may become blown quickly if plants experience drought or physical damage.

Bog plant Species which has evolved to grow in permanently damp soil. Such plants are adapted to these conditions and will wilt if the soil is allowed to dry out.

Bole The part of a tree trunk from ground level up to the first main branch.

Bolt To flower and produce seed prematurely. This is a particular problem in vegetable crops that are grown from their compact heads of leaves, such as cabbage and lettuce. Bolting may be caused by sowing the crop too early or late in the season or by dry conditions at the roots. When experiencing poor growing conditions plants will bolt or run to seed. This is a natural response to the poor conditions as the plant is producing seeds in case it dies.

Bond pattern Term used to describe the pattern created by laying bricks or blocks in such a way as to form a regular design eg English wall bond.

Bonemeal Plant fertilizer made from ground bones and containing large quantities of phosphate which encourages good root growth.

Bonsai Japanese method of growing and pruning dwarfed trees in containers. Bonsai specimens are often handed down through the generations and may be hundreds of years old.

Borax Hydrated sodium tetraborate, a naturally occurring mineral which is used as a plant fertilizer to correct minor boron deficiencies.

Bordeaux mixture This is a chemical preparation made up of equal quantities of copper sulphate and quicklime, and used as a fungicide.

Border Strip or area of ground alongside grass, paving or a boundary which is used for growing plants. Borders may be mixed or given over to the cultivation of a particular group of plants, such as an herbaceous border or annual border.

Botany Term that describes the study of plant classification, structure, physiology and ecology.

Botrytis This is a fungal disease (grey mould) that causes the rotting of young and soft plant tissues, thus leading to the death of the plant. Incidence of botrytis may be increased if hygiene is overlooked, when fungal spores may transfer to other plants through the soil or in dirty seed trays.

Bottom heat Describes the warmth that is given to the bottom of pots, trays or beds of compost to encourage the rooting of cuttings or the germination of seeds. Bottom heat has been shown to be more important than air temperature in the rooting of cuttings.

Bracket Fruiting body of a parasitic or saprophytic fungus formed on the trunk or branch of a tree or shrub.

Bract Modified leaf, usually protecting the base of the flower. Most bracts take the form of small, green or brown structures but they may be coloured and petal-like in some species, such as poinsettia. Some bracts have become brightly coloured in order that they may perform the function of petals, that of attracting insects to the flower for pollination purposes.

Bracteole Small bract on the flower-stalk

Branch Stem arising from the main stem of a plant, usually woody and creating part of the framework of a tree or shrub. Also used to refer to the divided habit of bushy plants.

Brassica Member of the cabbage family.

Break Leaf or stem growth which is produced from an axillary bud. May also be used to refer to an unusual flower colour produced in a particular species which would normally produce a different colour. This may have been bred into the plant by hybridization through sexual reproduction or may occur spontaneously by some mutation in the tissues of the plant.

Briar Common name given to wild roses which may be used as rootstocks in budding. These plants are recognized by the fact that they have seven leaflets instead of the five which are normally possessed by most cultivated varieties.

Broadcast Used to describe a method of sowing seed or distributing fertilizer by spreading it evenly over an area. This method is particularly useful when applying base dressings of fertilizer to an area prior to seed sowing or planting and also for sowing grass seed. To apply seed or fertilizer evenly, the area should be divided up into squares, which makes it easier to put down correct applications.

Broad-leaved Trees and shrubs which bear flat, wide leaves rather than the needle-like leaves of conifers.

Broad spectrum Used to refer to a chemical pesticide which can be employed against a wide range of pests, diseases or weeds. Also used to refer to some lamps which produce light through most of the visible spectrum and are used to mimic daylight.

Bromophos Active chemical ingredient used for the control of insect plant pests.

Brutting Term used for breaking the strong, current season's shoots of cobnuts. The stems are left hanging on the bush to encourage the formation of flower buds.

Bud Condensed shoot containing rudimentary leaves and/or flowers. The whole shoot may be protected by bud scales. Apical buds are those found at the tips of shoots; axillary buds are found in the axil between leaf and stem. Crown buds are large flower buds found at the tips of shoots.

Bud drop Condition usually resulting from physiological factors which cause the leaf or flower buds to fall from the tree or bush. Bud drop is often caused by drought at the roots.

Bud wood Harvested piece of current season's stem incorporating unopened buds which can be used in the process of budding.

Budding The process of uniting a bud from one woody specimen onto the prepared rootstock of another or the same species. A form of grafting.

Bug Common term used to describe any non-flying insect, although it is also sometimes applied to flying insect pests as well.

Bulb Storage organ composed of a con-densed stem and swollen leaf bases which overlap to give protection and food to the embryo leaves, stems and flowers within. The development of a bulb allows the plant to overwinter underground where it will get some protection from frost and inclement weather.

Bulbil Bulb-like organ found in leaf axils or flowerheads which is shed from the plant as a propagule to grow into a new individual.

Bulblet Small bulb developing from the edge of the basal plate of a mature bulb.

Bulb fibre Coarse grade, often immature peat which is used as a well-aerated and drained compost medium for the formed cultivation of bulbs.

Bulky organic manure (BOM) Coarse manure used as a soil conditioner to improve drainage, increase water retention and add certain nutritional elements to the soil.

Bullate Characteristic blistering or puckered nature of leaves.

Burr Spined or prickly fruit usually borne in a seedhead. Also a woody outgrowth on the branch or trunk of certain trees.

Bush Generally used to refer to a small shrub or a form of training the tree to form a rounded head on top of a trunk 1m (3ft) or less in height.

Buttoning Formation of large edible buds in the leaf axils of Brussels sprouts.

C

Cactus Succulent, flowering plant generally characterized by having swollen, fleshy stems and spines. These plants have adapted to growing in dry conditions of desert or semi-desert, and possess water-storing stems and roots.

Calcareous Used to refer to alkaline soils which have formed on limestone or chalk and contain calcium carbonate.

Calcicole Lime-loving plant which thrives on alkaline soil with a pH greater than 7. Such plants can be grown on acid soils with the addition of lime.

Calcifuge Lime-hating plant which will not grow on an alkaline soil. These plants require a pH of below 7.

Calcium Chemical which is used as a nutrient by plants and is required for healthy tissues.

Calcium carbonate Commonly called lime, this chemical compound is used to adjust the pH of soil and is added as a soil conditioner to clay, to improve structure and drainage. Used most on vegetable plots to correct growing conditions.

Callus Mass of plant tissue produced to seal wounds in response to mechanical damage either by natural means, pruning action or in the formation of cuttings. Callus protects tissues from disease infection.

Calyx Whorl of protective sepals fused together which enclose the flower in bud before it opens. *- Usually green*

Cambium Layer of actively dividing cells, known as meristematic tissue, which increases the girth of plant stems and gives rise to the annual ring in woody stems. *Found between the rind (bark) & the pith of plants*

Campanulate Having a bell-like shape. Usually refers to flowers, hence the Latin name for the genus *Campanula*.

Cane Elongated, slender woody stem. This term is usually used to refer to the stems of bamboo, raspberries, blackberries and other hybrid berries.

Canker Term used to describe a wound on the stem of a tree or shrub, caused by mechanical damage or fungal or bacterial infection. Usually indicated by swollen bark and, in some cases of disease infection, by a thick sappy ooze.

Capillary action This is the process by which water moves up through small pores, against the force of gravity, as a result of surface tension. Evaporation from the surface of soil or compost causes water to move up from lower levels by capillary action.

Capillary matting Synthetic fibre mat which is used to draw up water by capillary action. Used for irrigating pot plants on benches and to maintain humidity around the foliage.

Capitate Having the form of a head or dense cluster. Used to refer to the shape of an inflorescence or seedhead.

Capping Formation of a crust on the surface of soil caused by compaction or water impact. Crust is formed by small soil particles filling the spaces in between larger particles; this impedes the drainage of water and prevents the emergence of seedlings.

Capsid bug Sap-sucking insect which injects a toxin into plant tissues. Damage appears as distortion of leaves, flowers or stems. Small brown spots indicate the point of initial damage.

Capsule Dry seed case, often containing many seeds, which splits open to disperse its contents.

Captan Fungicide contained in some hormone rooting powders.

Carbendazim Active chemical ingredient of some systemic fungicides.

Carbohydrate Organic compound of carbon, hydrogen and oxygen which is made in plant cells to provide the energy for growth and cell functions. Carbohydrates are produced as a product of photosynthesis and are present in plants in two forms – sugar and starch.

Carbon dioxide Atmospheric gas used, with water, to synthesize carbohydrate in plant cells by the process of photosynthesis. Carbon dioxide enters the plant through the leaves.

Carbon cycle This is the cyclical process in which the element carbon is used by plants and animals to build organic compounds in their tissues, passed on through the food chain and returned to the environment by respiration and decomposition.

Carnivorous plants Common name used to refer to those plants that obtain all or part of their nutrition from dead animals which are killed by the plant's entrapment mechanism and digested by the secretion of enzymes.

Carpel The female part of a flower containing the ovules. The carpel is normally formed at the tip of the flower-bearing shoot and surrounded by the other organs of the flower.

Caruncle Wart or protuberance near stalk of seed.

Cascade A series of pools placed at progressively lower levels down which water rapidly falls.

Catch crop Quick-maturing crop which is grown among slow-maturing crops to make maximum used of an area of ground.

Caterpillar Common garden pest, being the larval stage of a moth or butterfly, and causing severe damage to young leaves, stems and flowers by eating the tissues.

Catkin Flower spike, pendulous or erect, composed of bracts shielding stemless flowers, often without petals and of single sex. Most catkins are wind pollinated.

Caudex The stem base of woody plants such as tree ferns or palms.

Cauliflorous Bearing flowers directly from the trunk or branches of the plant, often without stems or leaves.

Cells Units of which all organisms, including plants, are made. Specialized cells are grouped together to form the different organs which comprise the plant and operate together for the functioning of the entire organism. In plants, most cells have an outer cell wall which gives support. Within this is a cell membrane which retains the cell contents.

Cellulose Organic substance made of sugar which gives support and flexibility to plant tissues. Cellulose is present in the cell walls of plants to give them strength and to maintain their shape.

Centipede Animal which is related to insects and spiders. The long body is composed of segments, each bearing a pair of legs. Centipedes are carnivorous and are not a plant pest.

Certified stock/seed Plants or seed which are certified as being free from certain pests and diseases.

Chafer Insect which as an adult beetle feeds on the foliage of trees and shrubs and as a larva or grub causes serious damage to underground plant organs, such as roots, bulbs and rhizomes.

Chalk Base rock giving rise to the development of characteristically alkaline soil above.

Chamaephyte Small, woody plant which overwinters by the formation of buds on the branches which are carried above the ground.

Chartaceous Applied to leaves or flower petals which are thick and paper-like in their texture.

Chilling This term refers to a cold treatment given to seed, bulbs and other plants prior to germination or forcing, which breaks dormancy. Chilling may occur naturally through the winter months or it may also be carried out artificially in a refrigerator or cold store.

Chitting Starting into growth before planting, (seeds, tubers, etc.)

Chimaera Mutant plant containing a blend of genetically different tissue, brought about by grafting or changes in young cells. Plant chimaeras may produce foliage and flowers of either or both parents as well as intermediate leaves or blooms which exhibit a blending of the characteristics of each type eg *Laburnocytisus adamii*, a chimaera formed as a graft hybrid between *Laburnum anagyroides* and *Cytisus purpureus*.

Chitting Pre-germination of seeds before sowing which involves moistening the seed to hydrate its contents and rupture the seed coat. Most seeds respond well to this treatment and produce stronger-growing seedlings with a better percentage germination.

Chlorophyll Green-coloured plant pigment which is responsible for the absorption of light for photosynthesis in plant cells. Plants appear green because chlorophyll absorbs all other colours or wavelengths of light.

Chlorosis The loss or reduced production of green-coloured chlorophyll in plant tissues, resulting in yellowing of leaves and stems. May be due to low light levels, nutrient imbalance or infestation by pests or disease.

Chroma This term describes the quality of colour or hue.

Chromosome Thread-like structures contained in the nucleus of a cell. Chromosomes contain the genetic information which dictates the characteristics of a particular organism. Each cell of a certain plant or species contains the same number of chromosomes. Chromosomes divide during cell division.

Ciliate Bearing a fringe of short hairs on leaves, flowers or stems.

Circinate Meaning coiled or rolled, like the frond of a fern, having the shape of a shepherd's crook.

Cladode Flattened stem, resembling and functioning like a leaf, thus carrying out the processes of photosynthesis and gaseous exchange.

Clair-voyée Hole in wall or hedge to create a view out of the garden into the surrounding area.

Clamp Mound of harvested root crops protected from frost and rain by a covering of straw or soil.

Claw The narrow base of a petal.

Classification Arrangement of all organisms, including plants, into groups according to common or shared characteristics. The most common is the binomial system.

Clay Term for soil particles less than 0.002mm in diameter. A clay soil is one containing more than 25 per cent clay particles. Such soils are slow to warm up in spring and may be waterlogged in winter. They are nutrient-rich and are able to retain water during periods of drought.

Cleft Used to describe leaf structure which is deeply cut around large lobes arising from the main vein.

Cleistogamy Self-fertilization of a flower before opening.

Climate Term referring to the prevailing conditions relating to temperature, precipitation and humidity of a particular place. Macroclimatic or regional conditions are affected by large-scale factors, such as latitude, continentality, ocean currents etc; microclimatic conditions, those which affect a small area, are governed by aspect, soil type, vegetation cover etc.

Climber Plant which extends its shoots upwards to cover a support or another plant. There are a number of methods which plants use to climb, including scandent stems, twining stems, tendrils, thorns, aerial roots and sticky pads. Some climbers are self-supporting, others require support in the form of another plant or a man-made trellis or system of wires.

Cloche A domed or hooped structure made of glass or plastic attached to a frame, used to protect soil or crops from cold and wet conditions.

Clod Aggregate or lump of earth formed of soil particles.

Clone Genetically identical plants produced by asexual reproduction or vegetative propagation. Plants which are produced from cuttings are called clones.

Clove Small bulb section which forms part of the larger bulb eg garlic.

Club root Fungal disease prevalent on acid soils and affecting the roots of brassicas and crucifers causing them to become swollen and gnarled.

Cobble Large, rounded stone used as a decorative surfacing material. May be set in sand or concrete.

Coir Composted organic material made from coconut fibre. Used as a constituent of peat-free compost, a soil conditioner or surface mulch.

Cold frame Box-like structure with a glazed lid used to protect plants from cold and damp.

Cold stratification Cold treatment given to seeds to encourage germination. It may be used to break seed dormancy. The process involves chilling the seed in a fridge at 1–5°C (32-41°F) for up to 12 weeks until germination begins.

Coleoptile The sheath which covers the growing tip of grass stems.

Collar Part of a plant where the stem becomes the root. Also the ridge of bark where one branch joins onto another or onto the trunk.

Colour wheel Arrangement of colours in a circle, based on the primary colours.

Column Fused stalk bearing male and female organs in a flower. Mainly found in orchids.

Compaction Destruction of soil structure by heavy loads on the surface or by continued cultivation at one level in the soil.

Companion planting Close planting of species which are deemed to have a beneficial effect on the growth of other species. Such plants may release nutrients to encourage healthy growth or they may protect other plants from pest infestation.

Compatibility The condition which allows two plants to breed with each other, by the processes of pollination and fertilization, to produce seed which will germinate into viable new plants.

Composite Type of inflorescence where many small flowers are packed closely together in a head which gives the overall appearance of one single, large flower, such as in a daisy.

Compost This is a potting medium that is made from a mixture of materials to create an optimum root environment for plant roots. Different formulations are used for potting, seed and cuttings, ericaceous subjects etc. Also refers to well-rotted organic material used for soil conditioning or mulching.

Compost heap Stack of dead organic material gathered together to undergo decomposition.

Compound Two or more similar units comprising a leaf, flower or fruit.

Cone Seed-bearing structure of conifers and some flowering plants, which is composed of hard bracts.

Conifer Primitive tree or shrub bearing needle–like foliage and naked ovules in cones. Most conifers retain their foliage all year round, although there are some deciduous types.

onnate Uni'ked similar parts

nnechve Portion of filament connecting

Conservatory Glazed structure with a *tope* timber or metal frame, usually attached to *to the anther* a building. Conservatories were first built to house tender plants, giving protection

from the cold and wet, although today they are used by many as an extension to the living space of a house. They may incorporate some form of heating and modern structures may be double glazed.

Contact action Applied to the process by which a chemical damages or kills an organism on contact. Most of these chemicals are deactivated on contact with the soil, so their effectiveness is limited to the opportunity of the formulation touching the required target.

Contorted Stems or leaves which are twisted or spiralled. May be due to infection by a pathogen or is a characteristic growth habit of the plant.

Contractile Used to describe roots, stems or seed–bearing structures which coil up, usually as a result of the drying out of the plant tissues. Contractile roots pull plants back down into the soil; contractile stems may be employed to bring seed-bearing structures down to lower level for dispersion; drying of contractile seed-bearing structures may have evolved for efficient seed dispersal.

Convex humped

Coppice To prune back to the base the current season's growth of woody plants in order to encourage production of vigorous shoots. Also used to refer to a group of trees or shrubs which have been pruned in this way.

Cordate Heart-shaped when applied to leaf form.

Cordon Method of training woody plants as a single main stem and usually carrying short flowering spurs along its length. Used as a space-saving method of growing fruit.

Coriaceous Tough or leathery in appearance.

Cork Tissue composed of dead cells, impregnated with suberin, a waxy substance that provides protection against decay and water, and forming part of the bark of a tree or shrub. Forms a useful protective layer against mechanical damage, fire, extremes of temperature and desiccation.

Corm Underground, bulb-like, storage organ made up of a modified stem base with a bud on the top from which the roots and leaves appear. A new corm is formed on top of the original one which then whithers away. *The corm is covered by scales formed from the remains of leaves from the previous season's growth*

Cormel Small corm developing from the upper surface of a mature corm.

Cormlet Small corm developing from the base of a mature corm.

Corolla Whorl of petals in the flower. Generally quite brightly coloured to attract pollinators.

Corona Trumpet or cup-shaped structure borne from ,or within, the whorl of petals (corolla) in some flowers eg daffodil.

Cortex Plant cells that form the tissue under the epidermis of stems and roots.

Corymb Flat-topped cluster of flowers or inflorescence, borne on stems arising one above the other from a single, central stem.

Cotyledon Seedling leaf which is first to appear upon germination. This leaf (or pair of leaves) starts to photosynthesize to produce energy for further growth.

Courtyard Enclosed area, attached to a house or building, formed by walls, fences or hedges. Usually has some form of paving and often planted to take advantage of the sheltered conditions created.

Crenate Term used to describe the shallowly toothed or scalloped edge of a leaf.

Crenulate Used to describe the finely scalloped edge of a leaf.

Crest Tuft of hairs or bristles found on some flowers.

Crisped Having a minutely waved edge on leaves or petals.

Cristate Exaggerated crest present on some leaves or flowers.

Crocks These are pieces of clay flower pot that are used to maintain a constant drainage over the hole in the base of a pot or container.

Crome Hooked tined implement used to break up clods of soil to create a tilth. Often made by bending the tines of a fork at 90° to the shaft.

Crop Any group of edible or ornamental plants which are grown for a particular purpose, either from seed or cuttings. Plants may be grown for their leaves, stems, flowers or fruit. Also used to refer to the process of growing plants on a area of ground or for the action of harvesting fruit and vegetables.

Crop rotation The practice of growing vegetable crops on a different plot of ground each year to limit the build-up of pest and disease problems and to make best use of the soil nutrients. Crop rotations are commonly performed on a three- or four-year cycle ie two or three years elapse before the same crop is grown on the same plot again. Longer rotations may be preferable where pernicious pests and diseases have become a major problem. ~~cross-pollination transference of pollen from one flower to stigmas of another~~

Crown The part of a plant, generally found at soil level, where the roots and stems join and from where new roots and stems arise. This term is also used to

describe the framework of branches of a tree or shrub at a point above the main trunk or stem .

Crust Hard surface on the top of soil formed by the action of rain in the absence of a mulch of organic matter or a canopy of foliage. Fine soils which are low in organic content are most likely to form a crust and this can prevent seedling emergence.

Cryptophyte Herbaceous plant which overwinters buds below ground.

Cuckoo spit A popular name for a small insect pest which attacks different kinds of plant. The larva sucks sap from the plant and covers itself with a protective froth-like substance.

Culm Stems of grasses, including bamboo, which are usually hollow.

Cultivar A particular form of a plant species which has been bred and main-tained by the cultivation techniques of gardening. Not a naturally occurring vari-ety but a cultivated variety.

Cultivate The term given to the practice of growing crops and plants in soil or compost. Also used to describe the breeding and/or nurturing of a particular plant. Referring to the tilling of soil in preparation for growing crops.

Cultivator Long-handled, tined implement which is drawn through the soil to loosen the surface, disturbing weeds and loosening any crust. Also used to refer to powered machines which pull tines through the soil.

Cuneate Having a wedge-shaped appearance.

Curd Dense mass of immature flower buds which comprise the heads of cauliflower or broccoli.

Cuticle Layer of waxy material secreted onto the surface of leaves and some stems to reduce water evaporation from the tissues.

Cutting Any piece of plant material which is detached from a parent plant for the purposes of vegetative propagation. Cuttings may be prepared from leaves, stems and roots.

Cutworm Caterpillar of the turnip moth which feeds at night on leaves and stems, often cutting through them at soil level, causing considerable damage.

Cycad Primitive group of plants related to conifers and bearing palm-like fronds of foliage.

Cyme Inflorescence which is normally flat topped and composed of several arching side branches arising from a main stem. A number of individual flowers may be carried along each of the stems which make up the cyme.

Cystoliths mineral markings in the leaves as found in the Nettle family

Cytokinins Plant hormone which controls cell division in plants. Cytokinins are included in hormone rooting powders.

D

Damping down The wetting of floors and benches in a glasshouse to increase the humidity and to reduce excessive temperatures. Damping down may need to be carried out at least once on hot days during the spring, summer and autumn when the heat builds up due to the green-house effect, when humidity levels are low and when ventilation is insufficient to maintain a circulation of cool, moist air.

Damping off The wilting and death of seedlings that is due to infection with fungal disease. Plants may appear healthy, but then they suddenly collapse and die. Protect against infection by applying fungicidal drench.

Daylength Hours of daylight or artificial light received by plants which may affect the growth or flowering response. Daylength can be topped up with artificial light or black-out material may be used to cut out daylight.

Short-day plants grow, flower and seed only if they receive fewer than 12 hours of light; long-day plants only if they receive more than 12 hours of light.

Day neutral Used to describe plants which produce flowers as part of their natural growing cycle unaffected by the daylength.

Dead heading This is the process of removing dead or dying flowerheads to prevent seed formation, encourage repeat flowering in some species and stop die-back into stems. Annual plants need regular dead heading to prolong their display; faded flowers should be removed from roses and other plants to encourage the opening of other blooms.

Deciduous Species which lose their leaves at the end of the growing season and put out new growth and foliage at the beginning of the following season. Some conifers lose their leaves at the end of the season, but the majority of deciduous specimens are broad-leaved.

Decompose To break down organic matter, releasing carbon dioxide and inorganic compounds by the action mainly of bacteria and fungi. This process is a necessary part of the carbon cycle and recycles nutrients for use by other plants and animals.

Decorative This term is used in horticulture as a common name referring to particular groups or divisions of plant species eg the decorative group of chrysanthemums.

Decumbent Term that is used to refer to a flower, stem, leaf or whole plant which is hanging or declining, usually with the tips ascending.

Decurrent Term describing organs, usually leaves, flowers or thorns, which extend down the stem of a plant.

Deep-bed system Bed used for the cultivation of vegetables and created by deep digging, the incorporation of manure and the addition of soil from the surrounding area to leave the surface of the bed raised. Such beds should be no more than 1.5m (5ft) across and not walked on, to avoid compaction. Crops can be planted more densely as the soil condition is improved.

Deficiency Name given to a condition of the soil or of plants which are lacking in nutrients. Deficient soil will affect the growth of plants; plants which are deficient in certain nutrients may show signs of ill health.

Defoliate To strip the leaves from a plant either by seasonal leaf fall, the action of pests or disease or, in cultivation, by hand or chemical means.

Dehiscence The process of splitting in a seed capsule to release seed.

Deliquescent Describing part of a plant which is broken up into many branches.

Deltoid Mainly used to refer to the triangular shape of leaves, generally where the base of the leaf blade is wide and tapers evenly to a point.

Denitrification The conversion of nitrates in soil or water to nitrites and nitrogen by the action of organisms such as bacteria. This process makes nitrogen unavailable to other organisms. Denitrification forms an important part of the nitrogen cycle which maintains the balance and availability of nitrogen in the environment as a whole.

Density The number of plants which should be planted in a certain area. This depends on the moisture-holding capacity and fertility of the soil.

Dentate Bearing outward facing teeth, generally on leaf margins or flower petal.

Denticulate Carrying minute, outward facing teeth on the edge of a leaf or flower petal.

Deoxyribonucleic acid (DNA) Acid which forms part of a chain of similar acids, joined together to form a molecule which makes up the chromosomes in the nucleus of the cells of plants and other organisms. The arrangement of these molecules dictates the genetic characteristics of the plant.

Derived Having come from a particular source. Used to refer to plant names which describe some aspect, trait or history of the plant. Also used to identify the composition and source of chemicals.

Derris Naturally-occurring, active chemical ingredient which is used as an insecticide.

De-shoot To remove some or all of the shoots of a plant. May be used to channel energy into a particular bud or shoot.

Determinate Used to describe an inflorescence where the top flower opens first and prevents further stem elongation. Other flowers in the inflorescence open on side branches.

Dew Moisture deposited from the atmosphere as it cools on the surface of warm objects such as grass, plant foliage, soil, paving, etc.

Dew point The air temperature at which water can no longer be held in gaseous form and will condense onto a surface.

Dibber Pointed tool, usually of wood, used to make holes in soil or compost for the insertion of seedlings, young plants, tubers or bulbs.

Dicamba The active ingredient of hormone weedkillers.

Dichlobenil Soil-acting, granular weedkiller that may be applied to the surface of soil to prevent the germination of weed seeds. Soil must be left undisturbed after an application.

Dichlorophen Chemical used to control moss in lawns.

Dichotomous Two contrasting groups of plants which differ in morphology, parentage, origin or other aspect. Also used to refer to features which are widespread on an individual plant.

Dicotyledon Flowering plant that is distinguished by its having two seedling leaves which extend at germination to start photosynthesis. abb. Dicot.

Dieback Death of parts of a shoot or shoot tips resulting from damage or disease. Dieback may occur where incorrect pruning has been performed thus leaving a budless piece of stem. In severe cases the shoot may continue to die along its whole length and cause the demise of the plant as a whole.

Diffuse Used to describe loose or widespreading foliage or flowers.

Digging Cultivation process of loosening or inverting soil to improve the drainage and aeration as well as to maintain the best conditions for soil organisms. It may also be used as a means of incorporating soil conditioning materials such as manure. Single digging involves cultivation to one spade depth; double or trench digging involves cultivation to two spade depths.

Digitate Arranged with separate parts arising from a single point.

Dilute To reduce the strength or concentration of a substance by mixing it with water.

Also refers to the resulting strength of the substance.

Diluter Equipment used to mix concentrate with a stream of water at a specific rate, for output through a hosepipe. The strength of the resulting solution may be adjusted by flow rate of water, rate of injection of concentrate or by strength of initial concentrate.

Dimethoate Active chemical ingredient in some systemic insecticides.

Dimorphic Two different shapes of the same organ on a plant, eg leaf or flower.

Dioecious Male and female flowers of a plant species being borne on different individuals. Pollen must be transferred from a male flowered plant to a female flowered plant for pollination, fertilization and, therefore, the formation of seed.

Diploid Having two sets of chromosomes forming the genetic information of a plant or other organism. Most plant cells contain two sets of chromosomes which are formed by exact replication. Pollen cells and ova (egg) cells contain a single

set of chromosomes which have the potential to combine at fertilization; this condition is referred to as haploid.

Diquat Chemical ingredient found in non-persistent, non-selective, general purpose weedkillers.

Disbud To remove a terminal or axillary bud from a plant stem. Removal of a terminal bud is usually carried out to break apical dominance and encourage side branching or spray flower formation; pinching out axillary buds channels all the energy of the stem into a single bud or flower. Each type of disbudding is used in the production of different chrysanthemum blooms.

Disc Flattened or domed centre of a daisy flower, composed of florets. The disc is usually surrounded by petal-like ray florets which gives the inflorescence the appearance of a single flower. Such flowers are called composites.

Disc floret The small flowers which make up the central part of the flowers of *Compositae*. These are surrounded by larger, petal-like, ray florets

Disease Infection by a pathogen which causes a serious deterioration in the health of a plant or other organism. The disease, in the form of a fungus, bacterium or virus, inhabits the tissues of the plant from which it derives nutrition. Some diseases may live on a plant exclusively, others may perform part of their life cycle on different host plants. Diseases are usually contracted as a result of the plant's being under some form of stress; well-grown plants are less liable to infection.

Dishing The creation of a shallow depression around the base of plants to collect water and allow it to soak into the soil rather than run off the surface.

Disorder Any disease or factor which causes a deterioration in the health or efficient functioning of a plant.

Dispersal The movement of seed, plantlets or pollen away from the parent plant to an area where conditions are more favourable for subsequent development, in the case of pollen for sexual reproduction. Dispersal may be carried out by a physical mechanism, such as wind, water or an animal.

Dissected Used to describe leaves or petals that are deeply cut into fine sections. They may be divided and sub-divided in their formation.

Distal Any part of the plant which is relatively furthest from the crown of the plant, the opposite being the proximal end. The term is used to differentiate between the ends of cuttings; generally

the distal part of a root or shoot is thinner than the proximal.

Distichous Used to describe leaves that are arranged in two parallel ranks on opposite sides of a stem.

Distributor Mechanical device, either hand held or pedestrian, used for the application of a solid chemical to an area of ground. It incorporates some means of controlling the rate of application.

Ditch Lateral excavation either to form a boundary or to act as a means of drainage on waterlogged soils.

Diurnal The duration of a day, often referring to the number of hours of daylight. Also used to describe flowers which open, or stems which move in response to daylight.

Divaricate Parts of a plant that are spread far apart.

Divergent Term used for plants or parts of a plant with a spreading form.

Divided Refers to portions of a single leaf which are separated down to the base.

Division Method of increasing clump-forming or suckering plants by dividing them into sections, each with roots and shoots. Division is best carried out when the plants are in a semi-dormant state and can be dug up easily. Some plants grow in sections which can be easily broken up in pieces; other plants make a mass of tissue from which the plant grows and these need to be cut into section.

Also the name given to the resulting sections of divided plant.

Dolomitic limestone Ground rock containing calcium and magnesium carbonate, generally used to reduce soil acidity.

Dominance Used in plant breeding to describe a particular characteristic which dominates over the characteristic of another plant. For example, a particular flower colour may be dominant over another, which would be referred to as recessive.

Dominant gene The gene carried on the chromosome in the nucleus of a plant cell which dominates over genes for the same characteristic on other chromosomes.

Dormancy Used to refer to the state of seeds which are unable to germinate until certain controlling factors have been overcome. Dormancy can be due to chemical inhibitors in the seed or seed coat, hardness or impermeability of the seed coat, immaturity of the seed embryo, chemicals which inhibit growth of the embryo, etc.

Dormant The condition of buds or seeds before growth begins.

Dot plant Generally a tall plant used as a focal point in summer bedding schemes. Dot plants are usually fast-growing annuals or perennials which are overwintered under glass and then planted out.

Double Flower with more than the usual number of petals.

Double working Technique used to grow a variety on a rootstock with which it would otherwise be incompatible, for example certain varieties of pear are incompatible with quince rootstock. It involves budding or grafting an interstock of a particular variety onto a rootstock, then budding or grafting the fruiting variety onto the interstock. The interstock will grow on the rootstock and is compatible with the fruiting variety.

Doubly serrate Leaf margin edged with alternate small and large teeth.

Downy Fine, soft hairs giving a felt-like appearance to leaves, flowers or fruit.

Drainage The passage of water through the soil. Natural drainage of a soil can be improved by the addition of coarse material to increase the pore spaces between particles. Land drains may be installed to take away excess water.

Draw hoe Cultivation implement which consists of a wide, oblong blade attached by a single, curved 'neck' to a long handle. Also known as a swan-necked hoe. This tool is used by pulling or drawing the blade through the soil surface to chop through weeds. It is also used to make seed drills by pulling the corner of the blade through the soil at the required depth.

Drawn Term used to describe plants or seedlings which have become elongated and pale in colour.

Drench The action of soaking a plant or its root area with either water or a chemical solution.
    Also used to refer to the solution itself.

Dressing A term that is used to refer to a preparation which is applied to the soil at a particular rate. This could be a fertilizer, compost or may even take the form of gravel or a mulch material.

Dressed stone Pieces of stone that have been shaped after quarrying to create a shape which is more uniform and easier to work with. Dressed stone may be very highly finished for fine building.

Dribble bar Short tube containing small holes which is attached, horizontally, to the spout of a watering can for applying chemicals in the form of a liquid. It allows even application.

Dried blood This is a by-product from the meat industry which is applied to the soil as a high-nitrogen fertilizer to encourage leaf growth.

Drift Applied to air-borne droplets of liquid which are carried away during spraying either of liquid feed or, more seriously, some sort of pesticide. Weed-killers are a particular problem as drift from the application of these could kill nearby plants. Reduce the risk of drift by spraying on a still day and by placing screens around vulnerable plants.

Drill Straight furrow in the soil in which seeds are sown. May be created by using a stick, the corner of a rake or, for a wide drill, a spade.

Drilling The process of sowing seed in drills, usually applied to vegetable crops.

Drip irrigation System of watering which involves delivering water through small bore tubes or nozzles at a slow rate or drip which allows the water to percolate into the soil slowly without running off the surface. Drip irrigation applies water where it is needed and reduces the risk of wasteful evaporation from the soil.

Drip tip Pointed leaf tip which helps water run quickly from the surface of the leaf and down to the soil where it can be absorbed to supply the roots. Such leaves are found mainly on plants which grow in tropical rainforests.

Drupe This is a single hard–coated seed or 'stone' that is surrounded by a fleshy outer covering. *e.g. in plum*

Dry stone wall Functional or ornamental wall built using rough or dressed stone without the use of mortar, relying on the weight and interlocking nature of the stones to give the structure stability.

Dung Manure from animals used for soil improvement. Wherever possible obtain manure that has be allowed to rot before applying to the soil or it may damage the roots. Unrotted manure can be dug into the soil in the autumn if the ground is to be left unplanted until the spring.

Dust Chemical preparation in fine, solid form which is applied to plants or soil.
    Also describes the action of applying such chemicals.

Dutch hoe Cultivation tool consisting of a long handle on which a horizontal blade is mounted, held on two arms. The blade is used flat, in a sliding motion just under the surface of the soil to sever weeds and deposit them on the surface of the soil to wither. The D- or V-shaped space formed by the arms which support the blade enables the soil to pass over the upper surface of the blade.

Dutch light Type of glasshouse with sloping sides which are designed to maximize the amount of light entering the glass. Usually glazed with large panes of glass to minimize shading caused by glazing bars and the overlap of glass panes.

Dwarf Small form of a particular plant which is compact in one or all of its characteristics.

E

Ear Used to refer to the flower spike and seedhead of many grasses where flowers and subsequent seeds are held closely together at the tip of the stem, each floret bearing an awn or whisker-like structure.

Earth leakage circuit breaker Name sometimes given to a residual current device, an electrical component that plugs into the mains socket for electric power tools to be plugged into and which severs the electrical supply in micro-seconds if the circuit leaks to earth. This device helps protect against electric shock if a power cable is damaged in use.

Earth up The piling of soil around the stems of plants, such as potatoes and celery, either to encourage the development of tuber-bearing side shoots or to exclude light from the stems for blanching.

Earthworm Beneficial soil animal which feeds on soil matter and burrows through the soil helping to maintain an open, well-aerated structure. Earthworms are a good indicator of a healthy soil; their absence may suggest heavy compaction, poor drainage or soil toxicity.

Earwig Insect pest which feeds on the flowers and leaves of a number of decorative and edible plants both in its young and adult forms. Typical damage includes ragged holes in petals and leaves.

Ecology The study of living organisms, including plants, in relation to their natural environment.

Ecological niche A particular location where an organism can exist, taking advantage of the conditions which surround it. The organism is able to reproduce and function successfully.

Ecosystem Natural system involving organisms living in the environment. An ecosystem is controlled by biotic (living), climatic and edaphic (soil) factors, all of which interact to affect the cycling of nutrients in a food chain.

Ectotrophic Used to refer to certain mycorrhizal fungi which live in association with the roots of plants by forming a sheath around the root of the host plant.

Edaphic factors The effect which the soil has on plants or an ecosystem. Different plant species are adapted to growing on specific soils, which also influence the quantity and variety of other organisms.

Edging Trimming grass to produce a neat edge to a lawn and to limit the spread of grass into the border. Existing edges can be trimmed with edging shears which merely cut the foliage of the grass; the cutting of new edges or the redefinition of existing ones is carried out using an edging iron. Also used to refer to a narrow strip of stone, tiles, wood or plastic which is used to define an edge to grass, flower borders or paving.

Edging shears Long-handled, scissor-action shears with blades set at 90° to the handles, which are used to trim the foliage of grass at the edge of a lawn.

Edging iron Half moon-shaped blade attached to a shaft handle, used in a vertical slicing motion to cut through turf when marking out a new bed or redefining an existing edge to a lawn.

Eelworm Microscopic worms which cause considerable damage to herbaceous plants, bulbs and vegetable crops. Control of eelworm is very difficult and infected plants should be destroyed. Obtain healthy plants when buying and avoid planting the same crop on infected soil.

Electronic leaf Device used to control the rate of mist application on a mist propagation unit. Water evaporates from the surface of the electronic leaf at a similar rate to that from the foliage of the plants that are being propagated. When the device is dry, it triggers the mist unit to spray the foliage, thus keeping the plants moist and reducing the chance of their wilting.

Elliptic Leaf shape which is widest half way along the leaf and tapers evenly to a point at each end.

Elongate Foliage or stems which are long and often narrow.

Elongation Name given to the lengthening of stems, roots or leaves as a result of cell division at the growing tip. Mature structures are unable to elongate once the tissues have thickened.

Emarginate Leaf tip which is notched instead of pointed.

Emasculate To remove the anthers from a flower before the pollen has been shed. This prevents self-pollination and is used in plant breeding to stop self-fertilization and thus maximize the genetic variation of the offspring produced.

Embryo Immature plantlet contained within a seed. Usually possess cotyledons or seed leaves, rudimentary stems and roots. The embryo contains sufficient food for germination, either in the form of cotyledons or endosperm. The embryo develops by repeated cell division of the fertilized ova or zygote.

Emergent Water plant which has its roots and some of its stems under water, but sends stems, leaves and flowers up above the surface.

Emulsion A mixture of oil-based chemical and water applied as a pesticide to the trunk and branches of trees and shrubs.

Endemic Plant or other organism which is only found naturally in one specific area or region.

Endocarp Tissue that is contained at the centre of a fruit and which carries the seeds. The endocarp may contain high levels of sugar or growth inhibitors which will prevent the germination of the seed until they are broken down or washed from the seed coat.

Endosperm Mass of tissue present inside some seeds which acts as a food supply for the embryo plant until the cotyledons have emerged and can start the photosynthesis of sugar for subsequent growth. Non-endosperm seeds normally have large cotyledons which act as a food store.

Endotrophic Used to refer to certain mycorrhizal fungi which live in association with the roots of plants by growing directly from the cells of the host.

Entire Leaf which does not have lobes, teeth or hairs on its edges. The margins of entire leaves are smooth.

Entomophily Insect pollination of flowers. Such flowers are usually brightly coloured, with large petals and are often scented.

Bee-pollinated plants produce vast quantities of pollen which these insects collect; flowers which are pollinated by butterflies, moths or other animals produce nectar to encourage them to feed and to transfer pollen in the process.

Entomology The scientific study of insects, their morphology, life cycles and classification.

Environment The surroundings of a plant or other organism which include living (biotic) and non-living (abiotic) factors as well as events that happen in the surroundings, such as climate. The environment affects the growth and processes of plants.

Enzyme Protein which controls certain chemical processes in the cells of plants and other organisms. More than one enzyme may be necessary for a particular process. Enzyme action is dictated by environmental factors, for example temperature, and by the presence of co-enzymes.

Ephemeral A plant which completes its life cycle in a very short period of time. Some plants are able to germinate, grow, flower, set seed and die in a few months which allows a number of generations to be completed in a single season. Many species considered to be garden weeds are ephemeral.

Epicarp Also known as the exocarp, this is the outer layer of tissue in a fruit. It is often firm and skin-like to protect the contents of the fruit during dispersal.

Epicormic shoots Growths which develop from dormant or adventitious buds in the trunks or branches of woody trees and shrubs. Also called water shoots.

Epicotyl Stem-like structure above the cotyledons in a seed which extends to support the first set of true leaves in the developing seedling. The epicotyl emerges first in plants which exhibit hypogeal germination, leaving the cotyledons below the soil. In plants which show epigeal germination, the cotyledons are lifted out of the soil on the hypocotyl and the epicotyl develops above the seed leaves.

Epidermis Layer of cells which form the outer layer or skin of tissue on flowers, stems, leaves and roots of plants. The epidermis helps to maintain the shape of these organs and reduces water loss from the tissue. Spaces (stomata) in the epidermis allow air to pass in and out of the tissues and these are most numerous in the leaf.

Epigeal Form of germination in which the cotyledons are lifted out of the seed coat and pushed up above the surface of the soil, supported by a stem-like structure called the hypocotyl. The cotyledons

start to photosynthesize, producing sugars to support subsequent growth.

Epigynous Used to describe the structure of a flower where the gynaecium is contained within the receptacle at the base of the flower with the other whorls of floral parts attached to the top. The style of the gynaecium extends up the middle of the flower to support the stigma in a prominent position.

Epiphyll Plant which grows on the leaves of other plants where it can obtain light and moisture. Most of these plants occur in tropical climates, such as rainforests.

Epiphyte Non-parasitic plant which grows on the branches of other plants simply for support. No nutrition is obtained from the host with the epiphyte gaining water and dissolved minerals through its fleshy leaves and aerial roots. Examples of epiphytes include orchids and bromeliads from tropical climates, but there are many other plants which grow epiphytically where humidity is high.

Epsom salts Preparation of hydrated magnesium sulphate used as a source of the micronutrient magnesium to correct deficiency in plants.

Erect Referring to branches, leaves, inflorescences or individual flowers which are held upright.

Ericaceous Plant of the *Erica* family, the majority of which are lime-hating and need to be grown on a soil with a pH of less than 6.5. Also used to refer to a compost which has an appropriate pH for the healthy growth of ericaceous plants.

Espalier Form of tree or bush training. The main stem of the plant is grown up and side branches are trained out horizontally on either side, in a single plane. This method of training is often used for fruit trees or bushes grown against a wall, fence or framework when trying to save space in the garden.

Ethene Also known as ethylene, this simple plant hormone affects the abscission of leaves and ripening of fruits as well as other processes in the plant. Ethene given off any ripe fruit will encourage green ones to mature.

Etiolated Over-lengthened shoots caused by insufficient light combined with warmth. Deliberate exclusion of light is employed when forcing crops, such as rhubarb, for succulent, early pickings.

Etiolation The process of stem elongation which is caused by rapid cell division at the top of shoots.

Eutrophic Habitat which is rich in nutrients for the growth of plants or other organisms. Such rich growing conditions may produce excessive vegetation or populations of plants which are prone to pests and diseases.

Eutrophication Process which may occur in ponds, lakes and rivers when the addition of extra nutrients causes heavy algal growth, especially when the nutrients are nitrogen-rich. Having used up all the nutrients, the algae die and, in the process of decomposition by bacteria, the oxygen in the water is used up so that aerobic organisms cannot survive. This is a problem in garden ponds which may experience an algal bloom when nutrient-rich tap water is used to fill it.

Evaporation Conversion of water molecules from liquid to gaseous state which are then borne into the atmosphere. Evaporation takes place from the surface of any body of water: the epidermis of plants and other organisms and the soil. The rate of evaporation is affected by temperature, humidity and air movement.

Evapotranspiration The process by which plants lose water from the surface of their stems and leaves by evaporation.

Evergreen A plant which retains the majority of its leaves throughout the year, a proportion of which are shed when they have become old or shaded heavily by other foliage. Some broad-leaved and the majority of coniferous plants are evergreen. Also a common name which is used to refer to conifers in general.

Everlasting flower Common term used to refer to the cut blooms of certain plants that are composed of paper-like petals or bracts and which can be easily air dried for use in long-term flower arrangements. Most species grown for drying are either annual plants or herbaceous perennials.

Evolution Changes in the morphology and function of plants or other organisms over many generations, usually in response to the surrounding environmental conditions. Evolution occurs by the natural selection of the varied individuals which are produced by sexual reproduction and spontaneous mutations.

Excrescense Projection or protruberance from the main body of the plant. May be caused by infection with a pathogen or a physiological disorder of the plant.

Excretion Waste material or excess compound secreted by leaves, stems or roots of a plant as a means of eliminating them from the tissues where they may be toxic.

Exfoliate To peel off in layers, as in the bark of certain trees.

Exine The outer coat of a pollen grain which protects its contents during the transference from anthers to stigma. This coat is patterned in a way which is unique to a particular species and this characteristic can be used to identify and classify different plant groups.

Exocarp Also known as epicarp, this forms the outer layer of tissue in a fruit. Firm and skin-like, its function is to protect the contents of the fruit during dispersal.

Exotic Term used to describe a species of plants from a warm climate which is cultivated in a cooler climate. Such plants often require frost protection.

Also used to refer to plants with large colourful foliage or flowers.

Explant This is a tiny piece of plant tissue which is prepared and placed in sterile conditions for the purposes of micropropagation. Cells in the tissue undergo a rapid division and therefore differentiate into rudimentary roots, stems and leaves.

Exserted Referring to part of the flower which projects beyond another part.

Exstipulate Having no stipules or leaf-like structures at the base of the leaf petiole.

Extant Refers to a plant or other organism which is widely distributed throughout an area or region.

Extinct Plant or other organism which has been lost from a particular area, region, ecosystem or globally.

Extrafloral Organ which is positioned away from the flower.

Exudate Substance which is secreted by the tissues of a plant. May be naturally occurring or produced as a result of infection with a pathogen.

Exude To produce a liquid or substance from pores or from a cut surface. Water may exude from the leaves of some plants; this is called guttation. Sap exudes from cut or damaged parts of plants.

Eye Undeveloped or immature growth bud generally found on tubers and rhizomes.

Also used to refer to the centre of a flower, particularly if it is of a noticeably different colour.

F

F_1 hybrid Term applied to a seed strain that is produced by crossing pure breeding varieties, which gives rise to plants of greater vigour and with a higher degree of uniformity than open pollinated forms.

F_2 hybrid Seed strain produced as a result of self- or cross-fertilizing F_1 hybrids which are less uniform than the parents.

Fairy ring Ring of fruiting bodies (maybe in the form of toadstools), or discoloration in a turfed area which indicates the extent of the growth of the fine threads which form the underground network of a fungus. Discoloration in the turf is caused by exhaustion of the nutrients in the soil by the fungus.

Falcate Term applied to the form of sickle-shaped or curved leaves.

Fallow Technique of leaving an area of ground uncultivated for a period of time to allow for the development of improved soil structure or to reduce the risk of pests or diseases transferring to new plants.

Falls Hanging or horizontal petals of some flowers, such as the iris.

Family Term used in the classification of plants and other organisms to refer to a category or group of related genera. Plants are grouped together according to like characteristics, such as flower structure, morphology, etc.

Fan-shaped Term used to describe composite leaves which may be joined along all or part of their margins to form a wide fan-like structure, such as the leaves of certain palms.

Fan trained Form of training trees and shrubs, particularly fruit, where branches are spaced equally in a radiating pattern from a single trunk or stem. Plants are trained against a wall or fence in order to reduce the amount of space taken up in the garden.

Fancy Used to describe a flower which is unusually patterned, coloured or fringed.

Farina Flour-like meal which coats certain plant organs such as leaves, stems, flowers or fruits.

Farmyard manure (FYM) Bulky organic matter generally composed of the waste from farm animals and, in some cases, litter or animal bedding material. Used as a soil conditioner.

Fasciation Condition of stems or flowers where a number of organs or structures are fused together in a broad, flattened form. May be due to some physiological abnormality in a plant or infestation by a pathogen. Some fasciated plants have been brought into cultivation for their decorative quality.

Fasicle Term used to refer to a dense cluster of stems or flowers.

Fastigiate Form of plant, usually a woody tree or shrub, which is upright with narrow-forked branches or stems which create a columnar effect.

Feathered A young standard tree which has lateral shoots on the main stem. These shoots are pruned back by half in the first winter after they have grown and will help to feed and thicken the main stem. In the second winter the feathers are removed back to the base to leave the trunk clean.

Feed Common term used to refer to a fertilizer containing plant nutrients which is applied as a liquid or solid. Foliar feeds are sprayed onto the leaves of a plant in liquid form. A range of different fertilizers are available containing particular formulations of nutrients according to the differing requirements of particular plants or crops.

Fence A structure which is built to mark a boundary or to sub-divide an area. Wooden fences consist of upright posts which support either prefabricated panels or two or more horizontal rails, with or without thin strips of featherboard attached. Metal and plastic fences can be erected using wood, concrete, metal or plastic posts.

Fenestrate Having perforations, holes or transparent areas, usually in plant leaves.

Fenitrothion Active ingredient used as a plant pesticide.

Fern Group of green plants which are classified in the division pteridophyta. Individual leaves of ferns are borne along each side of a main stem, called a frond, which unrolls as it grows up from the crown of the plant. Fronds are often finely divided. Ferns may be herbaceous or in some cases tree-like. These plants do not produce flowers and reproduction occurs through two stages; spores are released from the underside of the frond and these germinate to produce a green structure called a prothallus which bears male and female organs. Fertilization occurs on the prothallus and the new ferns grow from this.

Ferrous sulphate Chemical used as the active ingredient in lawn sand to kill moss.

Fertile Plant which is able to reproduce sexually. Also used to refer to soil or an area of ground which is capable of sustaining healthy plant growth.

Fertilization Fusion of male and female gametes, that is the sex cells produced by the plant. In flowering plants the male gamete in the form of the pollen grain grows into the female gamete or ovum. The contents of each sex cell then mix and the two nuclei containing the genetic information fuse to form the zygote which will develop into the seed.

Fertilizer Chemical or group of chemicals which are applied to plants to provide them with nutrients. Simple fertilizers contain one chemical nutrient and are usually applied to correct a specific deficiency or to encourage a particular type of growth; compound fertilizers are composed of a number of chemicals and provide more than one plant nutrient. Balanced fertilizer provides equal amounts of the main plant nutrients nitrogen, potassium and phosphorus.

Fibre Strong, string-like tissue found in plants which helps to hold them together. Fibres are composed of long cells joined together, the cell walls of which are thick. Fibres are often elastic, therefore allowing the plant to bend and flex, or impregnated with lignin, which causes them to harden into wood.

Fibre fleece Synthetic, spun material which is woven into sheets and used to insulate vulnerable plants from frost by trapping a layer of warm air around the stems and foliage. This is useful for young seedlings or plants which have been planted out from a glasshouse, as well as for creating a tent–like structure around half–hardy plants in winter.

Fibrous roots Fine roots which are produced in masses from the crown of herbaceous plants, from the main woody roots of trees and shrubs or from the underground parts of the plant such as tubers, tap roots, etc. The roots are normally produced in the upper part of the soil and are able to take up water and nutrients. They provide only limited support to the plant.

Filament The stalk of the stamen in a flower. It supports the anther, usually holding it away from the flower where it can release its pollen.

Filiferous Divided up into many fine units. Used to describe leaves or stems.

Filiform Term that is used to refer to stems or foliage which are thread–like or long and thin.

Fimbriate Having a fringe, usually to the edge of leaves or flower petals.

Fire Condition in which leaves change colour through red to brown, usually caused by infection with a fungal disease. Most common on daffodils and tulips, it

will kill plants and can easily spread through the soil to other plants.

Fireblight Bacterial disease affecting certain trees and shrubs in the family *Rosacaea*, including *Malus*, *Sorbus*, *Pyrus*, etc. The disease enters the plant through the nectaries of flowers causing them to turn black and to wither; unchecked, it can spread down the stems causing the death of whole branches and eventually the entire plant. The disease can be spread by pollinating insects which visit the flowers for nectar.

Firming The action of compressing or compacting soil or compost around the root system of a plant to give it support. Firming is also carried out on freshly dug soil to consolidate the structure and create a stable surface for a seed bed.

Fish meal Dried and ground fish used as a fertilizer for plants. Usually formulated with blood and bonemeal to provide a high nitrogen and phosphate feed which will then encourage healthy root and shoot growth.

Flaccid Term used to describe the condition of plant cells which have lost water and have become soft. Plant tissues are composed of cells which, when full of water, press against each other to keep the plant upright. When cells become flaccid, the whole plant will start to show signs of wilting.

Flag Type of iris which has rhizomes and not bulbs. Also used to refer to flat paving units, usually of stone. Sometimes used to describe the wilted condition of plants.

Flagstone Flat paving unit of stone or pre-cast concrete which is used to create a hard surface on a path, patio or terrace.

Flail Machine used for cutting long grass, broad-leaved plants and shrubs. Metal blades are attached to chains and mounted on a rotating shaft. The turning shaft throws the blades out in an arc at such a force as to cut through foliage and plant stems. Machines can be used to cut rough areas of grass, verges and farm hedges.

Flame gun Gas or spirit burner which produces a flame that can be used to burn off the foliage and stems of plants. Used to clear areas of weed top-growth.

Flat American term given to a shallow seed tray or storage box.

Fleshy Generally used to describe the tissues of leaves, stems, roots or flowers which are plump and water filled. Such tissues are usually swollen by the volume of water which they contain.

Flexuous Meaning to have a wavy or zig-zagged edge or form. This term is used to describe the structure of leaves, flowers and stems.

Flint Hard stone-like material found buried in chalk rock. Used as a building material for walls and sometimes for paving. Water-washed flint gravel may be used as a path surface.

Floccose Relating to leaves, stems or flowers which are covered in clusters of fine hair or wool.

Flocculate Term given to the joining of soil particles into aggregates or clods by the action of applications of lime or the addition of organic material. This is a cultivation technique used on fine-particled clay soils to improve their aeration and drainage.

Flora General term used to refer to all types of plant life, although strictly meaning flowering plants.

Floral Relating to the organs of a plant which are contained in the flower.
    Also used to refer to any particular aspect of flowering.

Floral formula Notation used to list and enumerate the organs contained within a flower. Individual species have a distinct floral formula and this can be employed as a means of identification and classification.

Floret The small individual flowers which make up an inflorescence.

Floriferous Generally a plant which bears flowers. Used to refer to species which produce an abundance of flowers either massed at a particular time or over an extended period.

Floribunda Refers to the production of abundant flowers, usually held in clusters. Floribunda is particularly used as a group name for roses which produce a number of rose blooms at the end of each stem.

Floriculture The cultivation of plants for cut flowers.

Flower Part of the plant which contains the organs for sexual reproduction and the production of seed. Usually composed of sepals, petals, androecium and gynaecium, the flower may also contain nectaries and scent glands. Flowers are mostly adapted according to the method by which they are pollinated; insect-pollinated flowers usually have brightly-coloured petals and may produce nectar and scent; wind-pollinated species are inconspicuous, sometimes without petals, and have exposed stamens and stigma. Most species of flowering plants can flower only when mature; some plants die after flowering.

Flower bed Area which is used for the cultivation of plants for ornamentation.

Flower bud Rounded structure borne on branches which contains either a single flower or an inflorescence. The bud may also contain condensed stems and vestigal leaves or bracts.

Flower pot Cylinder-shaped container with tapering sides and a base for holding soil or compost in which to grow plants. Traditionally made from clay, flowerpots come in various sizes and some are plastic.

Flowers of sulphur Chemical used both as a soil acidifier and as a fungicide.

Flush Term used to refer to the production of shoots, leaves or flowers at a particular time.

Fogging Method of propagation which involves misting cuttings with very fine droplets of water that remain in suspension in the air for a long time thus increasing the humidity of the air without saturating the surface of the plants or the compost.

Foliage Term describing plant leaves.

Foliar feed Fertilizer containing plant nutrients which is applied in liquid form to the leaves of plants. Foliar feeds are quickly taken up by the plant and are particularly used to apply nitrogen for healthy leaf growth.

Follicle Either used to refer to a gland which secretes substances onto the surface of the plant or a dry fruit which opens on drying to release its seeds.

Folly Any sort of fantastic structure built in a garden or park, which usually serves only as ornamentation. Usually takes the form of a tower or gothic-style ruin.

Force To encourage a plant to come into leaf, stem growth or flower by the provision of warmth and shelter. Forcing is used for some vegetables, such as rhubarb, to produce tender stems for consumption. Bulbs are frequently forced for indoor flower displays in early spring.

Forest Large area of woodland comprising trees, shrubs and undergrowth. Often used to refer to an area which is planted with trees for the production of timber.

Forestry The scientific study, cultivation and management of trees usually for the production of timber.

Fork A division of a trunk or stem into two, similarly-sized parts. Also a pronged cultivation implement with a handle and used to refer to the process of cultivation of soil using a tined fork.

Forked Structure where a trunk or stem shows a division into two or more parts.

Forma A variant with a particular species which exhibits small but distinctive

characteristics which set it aside from the main species. It is denoted by a Latin name which follows the species name.

Formal garden Type of garden style where the layout of paths, borders and other features takes the form of geometric shapes when viewed from above. Also used to describe regimented or regular arrangement of plants in beds or borders.

Frame Box with a glazed cover which is used to protect plants and cuttings from excessively low temperatures or moisture. A frame may be heated or cold.

Also used to describe any structure which is used as a support for plants.

French drain Trench filled with coarse gravel or aggregate which is installed to drain surface water to a point where it can be discharged from the site.

Friable Used to describe an open, well-aerated and easily worked soil, composed of medium-sized particles which do not stick together and can be cultivated.

Froghopper Insect pest which feeds on young plant growths, producing a froth of sap around itself and causing distortion to stems and foliage. Commonly referred to as cuckoo spit.

Frond Term used generally to refer to any finely divided stem of leaves or flowers, but more specifically used as a name for the foliage units of ferns which unroll from the crown of the plant.

Frost The freezing of water as a liquid or as vapour when the temperature falls below 0°C (-32°F). Air frost occurs when air temperatures fall below 0°C (-32°F); ground frost occurs when soil temperatures fall below 0°C (-32°F). Fleshy leaves and stems are vulnerable to frost which causes the cells to freeze and rupture, thus killing them. Hardy plants are able to withstand frost.

Frost action The process of freezing followed by thawing of the water in the pores of soil or any solid object which breaks up the structure by virtue of the fact that water expands as it freezes. This action is used in the cultivation of soil where it is left to break down by frost action over winter.

Frost pocket Low-lying or dished area where freezing air collects and cannot drain away to lower levels. Frost pockets may be formed by the configuration of the ground or by solid barriers such as fences or evergreen hedges. The temperature in a frost pocket may fall below that of the surrounding area and frost may persist for longer.

Frost resistant Plant which is able to withstand temperatures which fall below 0°C (-32°F). Generally, young stems and leaves are least resistant to frost; mature, ripened stems and woody stems the most.

Fructification The process of bearing fruit or spore-producing bodies.

Fructose Simple sugar produced by plants and found in fruits.

Fruit The structure formed by the ripe fertilized ovary of a flower containing one or many seeds. Most visible forms of fruit include berries, hips, capsules and nuts which are formed by the ovary and sometimes the swollen receptacle at the base of the flower.

Also used to refer to edible structures around the seeds of some species.

Fruit bud Rounded structure on branches which usually contains one or more condensed flowers, that may produce fruit, and which may also include leaves and stems.

Fruit buds are generally plumper than leaf and shoot buds and are not generally sharply pointed.

Fruit cage This describes a net-covered framework used to protect fruit and vegetables from animal and bird damage.

Fruit set The point at which the fruit begins to develop, indicating that fertilization has been successful.

Fruiting body Structure produced by fungus which appears on plants or on the surface of the soil in order to bear spores.

Fumigate To disinfect or purify using the fumes produced by burning certain chemicals. Chemical fumigants are most often used to killed fungal spores, bacteria and insect pests in glasshouses, but some can be used to sterilize soil.

Fungi Organism which is unable to synthesize its own food and does not contain chlorophyll. Most fungi consist of thread-like structures which spread through the soil or in some cases over the surface of plants and obtain nutrients by saprophytic or parasitic feeding. A number of fungi are responsible for diseases of cultivated plants.

Fungicide Chemical used to kill fungi.

Furrow Drill or shallow trench which is used to aid drainage, for sowing seed or to expose the maximum area of soil surface to the action of weathering.

Fusarium Soil-borne, fungal disease which causes certain plants to wilt and die, a particular problem when plants are grown in the same soil year after year.

G

Gall Abnormal outgrowth from the root, stem, leaf or flower of a plant composed of tissue mass produced in response to infestation by a pathogen, such as insects, bacteria or fungi. Galls may cause some check to growth; most damaging are those caused by fungi.

Gamete Sex cell containing half the genetic information. In flowering plants the male gamete takes the form of a pollen grain and the female gamete the ovum.

Gamopetalous Used to describe a flower form in which the petals or corolla are joined to form a tube-like structure.

Gamosepalous Term given to the structure of the sepals in a flower where they are joined together along their margins to create a tube, often enclosing the base of the petals.

Gangrene Storage disease of potato tubers caused by fungal infection. Spores of the fungus enter the potato through wounds made when lifting the crop; tubers then rot in store.

Garden Area of cultivated land which is devoted to growing ornamental plants, edible crops or native species.

Garden centre Retail outlet for the sale of plants and garden sundries.

Garden design Positioning of the various elements which comprise a garden. The design and selection of plants is dictated by the physical and climatic influences. Various garden styles are recognized.

Garden line Length of strong twine, each end attached to some form of spike which can be pushed into the ground to keep the line taut. Garden line is used to mark out seed drills, planting rows and lawn edges.

Garden room An area within a garden which is enclosed in some way so as to divide it visually from the other parts of the garden.

Also used to describe a lean-to glasshouse or conservatory, usually attached to a house used for growing plants and as an extended living area.

Gazebo A small garden building or structure, usually with a roof and often with open sides from which to view a wide area. May incorporate a seat.

Gene Part of a chromosome made up of DNA, contained within the nucleus of the cells of plants and other organisms. Genes provide the information codes for particular characteristics and are borne in complimentary pairs which are separated in the formation of gametes (pollen and ova) and repaired at fertilization to provide the coding for the characteristics of the new individual.

Generation Group of plants or other organisms that are either at a similar stage of development or which have arisen as a result of sexual propagation. One plant generation can be considered as the time taken from germination until sexual maturity and thus the potential to produce a further generation; parents being one generation and their progeny the next generation.

Genetics The study of genes and the particular characteristics for which they provide the information, as well as the way in which genes are passed on through generations.

Genus Term used to refer to a group of related species. Each genus is given a Latin name which forms the first part of the binomial system of classification. Similar genera are grouped into families displaying common characteristics.

Geophyte A perennial plant which is able to overwinter by means of an underground storage organ, such as a bulb, rhizome or corm.

Geotropism Response of plant growth with respect to the gravitational pull of the earth. Roots are positively geotropic, growing in the direction of gravity; germinating seedlings are negatively geo-tropic, growing against gravity.

Germination Process by which seeds or spores develop into a young plant. In seeds the process of germination starts with the uptake of water into the seed and ends once the first true leaves form to take over photosynthesis. Germination is fuelled by stored energy.

Gibberellins Chemically complex plant hormones which control elongation of cells during growth and germination.

Gibbous The part of the plant which is swollen or protruberant at the base.

Girdling Removal or constriction of the bark that inhibits the flow of sugars from the top of the plant. Sugars are necessary for health and growth of the roots. Foliage above the girdling will remain healthy while it continues to be supplied with water from the roots, but once they die, the leaves will wilt and shrivel. Girdling may be caused by animal or physical damage or by constriction with a plant tie.

Glabrous Term used to describe part of a plant which is smooth or hairless.

Gland Group of cells, in the epidermis or surface layer of plant tissues, which secrete or excrete substances from the plant.

Glandular Referring to part of a plant or other organism which has glands or secreting cells. Such parts may be raised or slightly swollen.

Glasshouse Glazed structure used for the cultivation of plants which require some protection and shelter from extremes of climate, including temperature and moisture. Glasshouses may be unheated or cold; at the other extreme they may be heated to allow tropical plants to be grown. There are a number of different shapes of glasshouse, the basic forms of which are free-standing (with a pitched roof, sides and ends) or lean-to (using the wall of a building to form one side of the structure).

Glaucous Covered with a bluish, white or grey bloom on leaves, stems, flowers or fruit.

Gleying Blue-grey coloration at a particular depth in the soil, caused by waterlogging on clay soils.

Globose Spherical, usually referring to the shape of flower- or seedheads.

Glochid Small thin barbed hair which may be sub-divided and which is characteristic of many cactus species.

Glucose Sugar which is produced in plants and which makes up starch and cellulose.

It is produced by photosynthesis and is the basic form by which energy from the sun is stored.

Glume One of a pair of long, pointed outer bracts which are present at the base of each spikelet (flower) or a grass inflorescence. They protect the parts of the grass flower before opening.

Glutinous Used to refer to any part of the plant which is sticky.

Gnarled Any part of a plant, normally woody branches and roots, which is twisted, knobbly or distorted.

Graft To join one or more parts of a plant together to form a composite individual.

Grafting Process of artificially uniting a piece of plant material with another so that the tissues of each link together and continue to function for mutual benefit. Grafting is generally carried out using a rootstock and a scion which may take the form of a bud (budding), stem or branch. Grafting is used for species which have poor root systems and makes use of closely related rootstock plants which have desirable characteristics and which are genetically compatible. Plant material is prepared by cutting sections through the plant tissues of the rootsock and scion which are then brought together and bound to encourage formation of callus

material and thus the growing together of the tissues.

Graft hybrid Plant which has been brought about by abnormal growth which has arisen from a graft union. The resulting growth may bear some characteristics of the rootstock or the scion or it may have characteristic intermediate between the two. The best known example of a graft hybrid plant is *Laburnocytisus* (formed by growth from the union of *Laburnum* and *Cytisus*)

Graft union The point at which the scion or top growth is joined to the rootstock in a grafted specimen. This point is usually seen as a swelling where callus growth is healing the union.

Grain Used to refer to the seed of grasses. Also used to describe the particular pattern formed by the annual rings in woody stems.

Granular Soil structure which is composed of small regular particles, either naturally occurring or brought about by cultivation. Used to describe the soil structure of a well-prepared seed bed.

Grass An extensive group of monocotyledon, flowering plants, characterized by hollow, round stems with solid nodes at regular intervals. Leaves are narrow and strap-like, borne on a sheath which surrounds the stem. The flowers are carried in loose panicles, racemes or spikes.

Grassland Vegetation cover to the soil which is composed predominantly of grass and which gives rise to a particular ecology and habitat. A number of wild-flower species grow in a grassland habitat and these conditions can be emulated in the garden in order to successfully grow such plants.

Grease band Strip of paper which is covered in a sticky, oil-based substance for the entrapment of pest moths which climb up the trunks of some trees in order to lay their eggs.

Greenback Physiological disorder of tomatoes which is brought about by poor cultivation. Tomato fruits fail to ripen at the top.

Green bud Point at which buds turn green and begin to swell.

Green manure A quick-to-mature plant species which produces masses of leafy growth which can be turned into the soil to rot and provide organic matter and nutrients to the soil. Green manures are useful to grow over winter to take up and store nitrogen that would otherwise be washed from the soil and which will be released for other plants to use when the green manure rots down.

Greenfly Common, sap-sucking pest found on plants. These aphids feed by inserting their sharply pointed mouthparts into the tissues of the plants. They cause damage by reducing the vigour of plants, transmitting viral diseases and by the production of honeydew which attracts the sooty mould fungus.

Greenhouse This is the common name given to a glasshouse.

Greenwood Another term used to refer to softwood material which is used for cuttings, ie material that has not yet ripened or turned brown.

Grex Group of plants whose characteristics are so similar that it is difficult to differentiate between them. There may be a number of species or varieties of a plant which bear different names and yet appear to be the same plant.

Ground cover Term used to describe the planting of low-growing and spreading species which will cover the surface of the soil, in order to shade out weeds and their seeds. Also the name applied to any species of plant which can be used for ground cover.

Growing bag Elongated bag of compost, containing nutrients, into which plants can be directly planted through holes made in its surface. The bag which contains the compost is usually made of plastic to aid moisture retention.

Growing lamp Electric lamp which contains a light bulb or tube that emits light of a particular spectrum suitable for the growth of plants. Different wave-lengths of light induce varying plant growth responses. Such lamps are useful to encourage plant growth at times of low natural light and for inducing flower formation in certain species.

Growing point The tip of a shoot or root which contains actively dividing cells that contribute to the extension growth of the plant tissues.

Growmore Term describing a general purpose granular fertilizer which is for-mulated to supply equal quantities of each of the main plant nutrients – nitrogen, phosphate and potash.

Growth regulators Naturally-occurring or synthetic plant hormones which can be applied to cultivated plants to initiate a specific growth response.

Growth rings Concentric marks in the wood of trees and shrubs which indicate the annual increase in girth by the forma-tion of xylem vessels. The appearance of rings is produced by the size of the vessels; large vessels when the plant is growing quickly produce light areas in the wood, small vessels when the plant is growing slowly produce dark areas or lines.

Grub General name given to the larva of an insect, particularly those which are plant pests. Such larvae are often found in the soil and may cause severe damage by eating the roots of ornamental and crop plants. Also used to refer to the removal of plants, roots and stumps from the soil.

Guano Droppings of sea birds which are high in phosphate and are applied as a fer-tilizer to encourage healthy root growth.

Guard cells Pair of cells found either side of stomata which control the opening and closing of these pores.

Gumming The thick, sticky exudation which is secreted by the leaves, stems, branches or roots of some species. This may be a natural characteristic of the species or due to infestation by a pathogen. Continued production of such gum may result in the formation of large nodules of exudate and the condition should be investigated.

Gummosis Fungal disease of cucumbers, melons and marrows caused by inade-quate ventilation and heat.

Guttation Process by which water is forced out or exuded from the ends of the veins at the margins of the leaf. It is particularly noticeable during periods of high humidity in the atmosphere around the plant when water cannot evaporate from the leaf surface.

Guying This is a system of ropes or metal wires which are attached to the branches of newly-planted trees and shrubs, and are then secured in the soil to keep the plant upright.

Gymnosperm Sub-division of flowering plants which mainly differ from angiosperms in having naked or unprotected ovules and their reproductive organs arranged in cones. Conifers and cycads are both gymnosperms.

Gynaecium The female parts of a flower borne at the tip of the flower stalk. The gynaecium consists of one or more pistils comprising the stigma, style and ovules which are involved in sexual reproduction.

Gypsum Hydrated form of calcium sulphate which can be used to provide calcium to the soil.

H

Habit The shape in which a plant characteristically grows.

Habitat The environment in which a plant naturally grows.

Haft Another word for shaft, the narrow base of petals, such as those of irises; a winged leafstalk.

Can also be applied to tool handles.

Hair A modified epidermis cell which forms an outgrowth from the surface of a plant.

Half-hardy The term that describes a plant's ability to cope with fairly low temperatures (lower than 'tender' plants), but not frost.

Half-moon A tool with a long handle and a semi-circular cutting edge at the base, used for shaping lawn edges.

Half-ripe A stem cutting which is taken from the current year's growth during the late summer. The term refers to the point at which stems are beginning to change from the soft and therefore easy-to-break stage of growth, to the stage where they have become completely woody and hard-barked, such as those which are needed for 'hardwood' cuttings.

Half-standard A tree which is grown with a bare stem of 0.9-1.5m (3-5ft) with all of its foliage and flowers at the apex; it has a shorter length of bare stem than a 'full standard'.

Halide lamp Form of glasshouse lighting with the ability to illuminate a large area and which closely resembles natural light. It is used to increase light levels when day length is short, in winter and spring.

Halophobe Any plant which cannot tolerate very salty (seaside) conditions.

Halophyte A plant which is tolerant of, or has adapted to, saline soil conditions. This includes all plants which grow happily near the seaside, for example, rosemary (*Rosmarinus officinalis*), hebe, osteospermum.

Hamate Hooked, particularly at the tip.

Hand fork A tool with a short handle used to cultivate the soil.

Hand texturing A method of assessing the texture of a soil by moistening a handful of soil until it is sufficiently wet to hold the particles together. A small amount of the moistened soil is taken between finger and thumb and kneaded to break down the structure. If a soil is sandy it will feel relatively gritty; silty soil will feel 'soapy' or silky, while a clay soil will smear and produce a shine. The greater the clay content, the stickier the soil will feel and the greater the ease with which particles will hold together.

Hanging basket A semi-circular wire container for plants intended to be suspended indoors or outdoors. Lined with moss or other absorbent material which allows drainage, it is a decorative item for winter or summer.

Typical plants for a summer hanging basket include: trailing fuchsias, lobelia, helichrysum, Busy Lizzies (*Impatiens*); plants for a winter hanging basket might be: ivies, small heathers or conifers, winter pansies or perhaps Christmas cactus (*Schlumbergera*).

Hapaxanthic Having one flowering period.

Haploid The basic number of chromosomes possessed by the sexual cells of most plants.

Hand-light Dated term for a cloche.

Hard landscape The bricks, paths, walls, pergolas and so on which make up a garden or landscape, as opposed to the 'soft' part of the landscape, which is that made up of plants.

Hardcore A foundation made of rocks and stones above 2cm (¾in) in size, used as a base for paths and sheds, for example.

Harden off To accustom a plant (often grown from seed under cover) to outside conditions, usually colder than those it has been used to. Hardening off invariably takes place in late spring when plants are put outside in the shelter of a wall or cold frame for increasing amounts of time during the day. They will then be brought back under cover for the night, particularly when there appears to be the threat of a frost.

Hard prune To cut back a plant to within a few buds of the base to promote more vigorous growth. Plants which form buds on old wood, near the ground respond well to hard pruning, for example, buddleia and lavatera.

Hardwood cutting A cutting from a ripened stem of the current year's growth taken during the dormant season. The stem should be hard and rigid, and not obviously new growth.

Plants suitable for propagating in this manner are trees, hardy shrubs and also soft fruits.

Hardy A plant's ability to survive outdoors without the protection of glass. 'Hardy' is often used as a rather vague term, attributing general strength to a plant, but in fact describes a plant's ability to cope with the action of frost. (In very hot countries, it can be used to describe a plant's ability to cope with drought).

Whether a plant is pronounced hardy or not depends on the experience of the individual grower; many plants lie on the boundary between tender and hardy and it is the gardener's challenge to cultivate such plants successfully. Often the lure to do so lies in their uncommonness due to the fact they are more suited to other climates.

Harmonize/Harmony In garden design terms, colours next to each other on the colour wheel (spectrum) are said to harmonize. For example, blue, blue-violet and violet harmonize well. Also, harmony can be achieved by planting a tint, a tone and a shade of the same colour in close proximity. Carmine, pink and dusky rose, all shades of red, harmonize well.

Hastate A leaf shape rather like an arrow at the tip and rounded lobes turned outwards at the base.

Haulm/Halm What is left of vegetables after they have been harvested, for example straw and stems of plants.

Also used in reference to potatoes, beans and peas.

Haustorium The part of a parasitic plant which attaches to the host and via which nourishment is derived.

Haw The berry belonging to a hawthorn tree (*crataegus*).

H₂O The chemical symbol for water, a vital ingredient of every plant's health.

Head A group of flowers at the end of a stem, for example, hyacinth, allium, hydrangea. Accordingly, also the centre of a leaf vegetable, such as cabbage, cauliflower or lettuce.

Also used to refer to the branches of a standard or half-standard tree or shrub.

Head back / Head down Often used when referring to fruit trees, this is the practice of cutting back a tree or shrub to all, or some, of its dormant buds.

Heart The centre of a vegetable such as a lettuce, cabbage or cauliflower.

Hearting The stage of development when a leaf vegetable, such as a cabbage or cauliflower, begins to form a cluster of central leaves.

Heart rot Describes the decay of a plant's internal tissues.

Heart wood The hard, central wood of a tree; the duramen.

Heating This is of great importance to the gardener for a number of reasons: with its assistance tender plants can be raised; plants can be grown out of season; plants which resent damp conditions can grown; and the production of roots can be stimu-lated, particularly relevant in the case of striking cuttings.

Heating can be provided in numerous ways, including gas-fired boilers, electrical heaters, paraffin oil heaters and the old-fashioned method of hot beds.

Heave The action of frost on soil causes soil to 'heave'. When water in damp soil freezes, it expands and causes the soil to raise up, unearthing newly-planted plants.

Heavy Term that refers to a soil with a high clay content.

Hedge A series of plants, usually of the same variety and often evergreen, positioned at set distances to create a screen. This might be in a single row – between 30-64cm (12-25in) apart – or in a staggered double row which makes a good windbreak – planted 89cm (35in) apart.

Plants chosen for hedges are often evergreen, so that they create a year-round screen; they can also cope with being continually trimmed. Common hedging plants include holly (*Ilex*), privet (*Ligustrum*), and yew (*Taxus*) among others.

Dwarf hedges are more ornamental and are used for low boundaries to lawns and might comprise lavender or dwarf berberis, ground cover roses and so on.

Hedge trimmer A power-assisted or hand-operated tool for pruning and shaping hedges. Power may be electric, battery (even car battery) or petrol. Hand-operated hedge trimmers include short and long-handled shears.

Heel The piece of bark or stem which is retained on a shoot when it is taken for the purpose of propagation via heel cuttings.

Heel cuttings A cutting which takes the most vigorous side shoots from the stem of the parent plant for the purposes of propagation. Some plants, for example, perovskia, escallonia and berberis, are more able to produce roots if the heel is retained in this way.

Heel in The practice of placing plant roots (usually of trees) in soil before placing them in their final planting position. This might be necessary for bare-rooted plants, in particular, if the planting site is not yet prepared. In this way, plants have access to the necessary food and moisture while waiting to be planted.

To heel in, a v-shaped hole should be dug out, or a trench if more than one plant is to be heeled in. The end result should be that the plant isn't standing on its own roots but leaning slightly to one side. Compost and water should be added to enrich the site if it is very poor and then the plant's roots placed in the soil, ensuring that all are covered – none should be left sticking above the surface,

as they would quickly dry out and cause stress to the plant, making its establishment, once planted, more difficult.

Helically Like a helix; spirally, in the arrangement of a spiral.

Helminthoid Shaped like a worm.

Helminthology The study of worms.

Helophyte A plant which grows in mud, either seasonally or on a permanent basis.

Usually applied to plants which have culinary or medicinal uses, such as basil, feverfew or thyme, but also used as an abbreviation of herbaceous.

Herb bench A natural bench with the seat made from chamomile, usually the low-growing variety 'Treneague' which is sweetly scented. The sides can be made from brick or whatever material is preferred and then infilled with plenty of grit for drainage with the last 15cm (6in) or so filled with compost. It is best if the bench is sited in a sunny position.

Herbaceous Any plant without woody stems which dies down at the end of its growing season, having produced seed, including annuals, biennials and perennials. In common use, herbaceous is usually applied to perennials which die down at the end of the growing season and reappear the following spring.

Herbaceous might also be applied to a flower or sepals, meaning that they have the appearance of a leaf, either in colour or texture.

Herbaceous border A part of the garden which comprises solely herbaceous plants. The tradition of such a border originates from the early part of the nineteenth century. It typifies the English garden in summer, with its rich use of colour, sometimes in planting schemes but often simply riotous.

Herbaceous borders are best situated in full sun, as most suitable plants are sun-lovers and will fail to flower and become leggy if they don't receive enough light.

Herbal A book which contains descriptions of herbs and their uses. Many of these were written in previous centuries, notably John Gerard's *Herball* of 1597. At this time all medicine was derived from herbs so it was important to be able to identify and grow them properly.

Herb garden A garden which comprises only herbs. Commonly, herbs are planted formally in a particular shape, such as a cartwheel, parterre or 'knot' garden.

Herbicide A chemical or combination of chemicals used to kill plants – usually those considered weeds. Herbicides may be diluted and sprayed over an area, or specifically applied to weeds where other growth should not be damaged, for example, in a lawn.

Hermaphrodite A plant which has both male and female reproductive organs.

Hesperidium A fruit of the orange type which is pulpy with a tough outer skin.

Heterogamous Bearing two types of flower, such as the disc and ray florets of the daisy, or male and female on the same plant.

Also describes indirect pollination.

Heteromorphic Taking on different shapes from the norm at various stages of the life of a plant.

Heterophyllous A plant which has different kinds of leaves, possibly at the same time, for example, *Eucalutptus gunnii* in which the juvenile leaves are blue and round and the older leaves lance-shaped and green. Often these plants are regularly pruned to maintain the young growth.

Heterosporous The asexual production of spores of both sexes which develop into male and female gametophytes.

Heterostylous Flowers which differ in numbers, length or types of styles present.

Hibernaculum A winter bud or bulb, in which form a plant survives the winter and which becomes regenerated during the following spring.

Hilum The scar left on a seed at the point where its funicle (stalk) was attached.

Hip/Hep The ripened seed or fruit belonging to a rose.

Hippocrepian In the shape of a horse-shoe.

Hirsute Describes a plant covered in hairs or stiff spines.

Hirsutullous Slightly hirsute.

Hirtellous Very slightly hirsute, downy.

Hispid Describes a plant which is rough to the touch, or covered with strong hairs or bristles.

Hispidilous Very slightly hispid.

Histamine A substance present in the human body which is released into the bloodstream when a burn or wound occurs. Relevant to gardeners who suffer from hayfever as histamine comes into play when people have an allergic reaction to pollen.

Hoar frost The layer of crystallized water that appears on the earth's surface after a period of humid air, or dew, has been followed by freezing.

Hoary Describes a plant which is covered in white-grey hairs.

Hoe A tool used to cultivate the soil and rid it of weeds. Different kinds are available, for example, a draw hoe, Dutch hoe, onion hoe, triangular hoe or one with jagged edges which pulls the weeds out as it is drawn towards you.

The draw and Dutch hoe are the most commonly used: the draw hoe is is used by pulling it towards the body and is good for breaking up lumps and severing weeds in heavy soil, while the Dutch hoe is used by pushing it away from the body and back again while moving along a border.

Hoeing The practice of moving a hoe through soil to kill weeds by uprooting the seedlings. It is also done to thin out seedlings that are sown in rows and to draw seed drills.

Hollow heart A problem which sometimes occurs in potato growing, whereby the tubers are hollow at the centre. It is not thought to be due to insects, but to soil conditions, so good soil preparation is one preventative measure, especially when very dry.

Varieties which make very large potatoes are best avoided where this problem occurs.

Homochlamydeous Having a similar calyx and corolla.

Homogamous Having hermaphrodite flowers or flowers of the same sex.

Homologous Describes organs or parts that are alike in appearance or purpose.

Homomorphic Having the same shape.

Homonym During the botanic naming of plants, sometimes names are discovered to have been duplicated. This can be due to the botanist realizing that such a name has already been used or that a plant believed to be undiscovered has already been named. The same name used repeatedly in this way is known as a homonym.

Homosporous Producing only one kind of seed; or borne of only one kind of spore.

Honeydew A sticky substance found on the surface of leaves, secreted by aphids from the leaves of plants they are feeding on overhead. Very often this substance is found in conjunction with sooty mould.

Honey fungus *Armillaria mellea* affects the roots of trees and some herbaceous species, and is a soil-borne disease transmitted via spores. Symptoms include mushroom-like fungus at the base of the tree in autumn and bootlace-like, black strips under the bark. Hyphae travel underground and can infect nearby plants.

No cure is available so plants, together with their roots and surrounding soil,

must be removed. Rotavating the surrounding area repeatedly is thought to be one way of combating the problem once the stump has been removed.

Hood (hooded) A part of a plant which is like a hood, for example, the flowers of aconitum (commonly known as monkshood).

Hoof and horn A concentrated, organic fertilizer made of ground-down hooves and horns, comprising nitrogen solely, primarily for good leaf and stem growth. Its effects are slow acting, dependent on its breakdown in the soil by soil organisms. Weather therefore affects its activity – in cold weather such a fertilizer does not have much effect.

Hops Spent hops (having been used by a brewery) are used as a soil conditioner. Hops do not really contain much in the way of beneficial plant food. However, they are excellent for making heavy soils more workable.

Hop manure Hops which have been chemically treated to improve their value as a plant food. They are usually used as a topdressing in spring.

Hormone A natural substance which circulates in the sap of plants and regulates growth, bud and root formation. Also, an artificial growth regulator.

Hormone rooting powder A powdery substance used to root cuttings more quickly.

Horn An appendage or protuberance on a plant shaped like a horn.

Horny Meaning hard or calloused, but easily penetrable.

Horse manure A fertilizer made from horse dung. It has a dry and open texture, its water-retentive and fibrous properties recommend it and it's often used to provide the heat in hot beds and bottom heat.

Hort (Horti) Of the garden.

Hortorum Of gardens.

Hortulanorum Of gardeners.

Hose A conveyor of water, attached to a tap, for watering. Flexible, it can be made from rubber or plastic and may be perforated for watering along rows, for example, in the vegetable garden.

Most hoses are tubular, but some can be pressed flat, only becoming tubular when full of water. This prevents the irritating kinking which can impede the flow of water.

Hose in hose A description of flowers in which the petals are so arranged that they appear to be one inside the other.

Host A plant which is carrying a parasite, be it a pest or another plant, such as mistletoe (*Viscum album*), which obtains minerals and water from its host tree.

Hostile A term used of soils and climate conditions which are unfavourable for growing a plant. For example, the acid-loving rhododendron would find a chalky soil 'hostile'.

Hot water A treatment used to destroy pests in bulbs. Bulbs are immersed in hot water at a precise temperature for a period of time; a risky process, as if there is any variation in either time or temperature the pest may not be killed, or the bulb may be destroyed.

Hot bed A method of raising plants, especially tender ones, under glass, popular in Victorian times. This is done by incorporating fermenting manure into the soil, thus providing bottom heat and promoting growth. Hot beds under cold frames and cloches are particularly useful for raising early salad crops, such as lettuce and endive.

A modern day hot bed is created by installing heated electric cables under soil.

Hover mower An electric lawn mower with rotary blades which is held above the ground by jets of air from fans, or is simply raised up by the action of the blades spinning. These mowers are very light and provide much manoeuvrability in all directions; they are particularly good for mowing banks and other awkward-to-reach areas.

Hue In garden design terms, a 'hue' is a true colour. An example of a hue could be the colour red, for example. Add white and the result is a 'tint' (pink); add black and the result is a 'shade' (maroon); add grey and the result is a 'tone' (plum).

Hull The pod in which peas, beans and nuts are encased.

To hull To remove from this outer layer.

Humid (Humidity) The moisture in the atmosphere. A vital ingredient for plants, specially 'epiphytic' plants, or air plants, which derive water from the air rather than the soil.

Humus Organic matter which has been broken down by bacteria in the soil, resulting in a black, crumbly substance from which plants can easily resource food.

Hurdle A rural-looking fencing panel made of wood, woven at intervals through upright poles. The wood used is usually hazel or willow.

Husk The thin, dry outer skin of fruits and nuts, such as sycamore fruits.

Normally used to refer to the covering after the inside has been removed.

Hyaline Transparent or glassy. Normally used with reference to leaves and petals that are so thin as to appear see-through.

Hybrid A variety of plant resulting from the crossing of two different species or genera. Pollen is removed from a male plant of one genus or species and brushed on the stigma of a female plant of another.

Often hybrids do not themselves produce seed, and if they do, invariably the offspring will not have the appearance of its hybrid parent. Hybrids are usually shown as preceded by an 'x', for example, *Magnolia* x *soulangeana* is a cross between the magnolia species *denudata* and *liliiflora*.

Hybrid tea Two classes of roses in the nineteenth century – the hybrid perpetuals and tea roses – gave rise, via cross-fertilization, to the hybrid tea. The hybid perpetual provided vigour, larger flower size and fragrance to the cross, while the tea rose provided the recurrent flowering abilities and thick, glossy petals.

Hybrid vigour The increased strength of some hybrids (but certainly not all), displayed by neither parent.

Hydathode Also known as lime-dot, a water-secreting gland, rather like a stoma, situated in the epidermis.

Hydrated lime See lime.

Hydrophyte A plant which thrives in a waterlogged medium, more commonly known as 'aquatic plants' or marginals.

Hydroponics A method of soilless culture, which involves growing plants in a solution of plant nutrients.

Hydroscopic Expanding when water is present, and contracting when it is not.

Hygrometer An instrument for measuring the moisture in the air (humidity).

Hypanthium Also known as a 'floral cup', this is the fusion of the calyx, corolla and stamens into a cup- or tube-like structure.

Hypertufa An artificial form of tufa rock, with the same absorbent properties. It is made of one part cement: two parts sand: two parts granulated peat and then moulded to imitate a rock shape. Holes can be blasted out of it for planting rock gardens by spraying a strong jet of water at the rock.

Hyphae Stringy growths made by fungus.

Hypochile The lower part of the lip of some orchids.

Hypocotyl The part of a seed or seedling just beneath the cotyledons.

Hypogeal germination A type of seedling growth whereby the cotyledons remain below the surface of the soil instead of becoming cotyledon leaves.

Hypogynous Of the calyx, corolla and stamens, being held below the ovary, often on the receptacle.

Hysteranthous Of leaves which develop after the flowers.

I

Ichneumon flies Parasitic insects of the family, *Hymenoptera*, useful to gardeners because the females lay their eggs in caterpillars. The larvae, when they hatch, consume their host.

Idioplasts Epidermal cells which produce gum or slime.

Illite A pale-coloured clay mineral found in shales and sediments.

Imbricate Plant tissue that is laid closely overlapping, like scales, for greater strength or protection. For example, the branches of the monkey puzzle tree, *Araucaria araucana.* & *lily (lilium) bulbs.*

Immersed Of features which are sunken underneath the surface of a leaf.

Immortelle An 'everlasting' flower, one which has been dried, such as helichry-sum flowers or dried poppy (papaver) seedheads. Taken from the French word for immortal.

Immune/Immunity Plants which are able to overcome life-threatening pests and dis-eases are described as immune. Some plants are more susceptible to a particular pest than others so breeders pay special atten-tion to creating some sort of immunity.

This term should not be confused with resistant, where plants and indeed pests are able to *fend off* trouble but may eventually succumb.

Immunology The study of plant and animal ability to become immune to pests and diseases.

Immutable Unchangeable.

Imparipinnate This term describes where a compound pinnate leaf terminates with a single leaflet.

Imperfect The description used when parts of plant that are normally present have not developed.

Impermeable Describes a substance which does not allow the passage of fluids.

Implant To engraft or insert; or, when used as a noun, a graft.

Impressed Embedded in the surface (of a leaf or petal etc).

Inarching A kind of grafting without separating the stem of either plant from its individual roots until the graft has successfully taken.

Inbred The result of inbreeding, as happens when a bisexual flower pollinates itself.

Incinerator Any apparatus for burning garden rubbish. Preferably only diseased garden rubbish and very woody debris that won't break down easily into compost should be burnt.

Incised Refers to leaf margins which are sharply toothed, as if cut with pinking shears.

Inclined Leaning forwards or backwards, particularly of a flower on a stem. An 'inclined' dahlia would be disqualified from a show.

Included Not protruding but enclosed within. For example, stamens are enclosed within a corolla.

Incomplete Of a flower which has one of its four whorls missing.

Inconspicuous Not conspicuous or particularly noticeable. Plants, such as leucothoe, are said to have 'inconspicuous' flowers. It is not that they are particularly unattractive, simply rather small and so the plant is grown for another specific reason, such as for its textural value or foliage colour.

Incrassate Thickened; usually describing an epidermis.

Incumbent Resting its weight on a separate support or organ.

Incurved A term applied to flowerheads, such as those of chrysanthemums, whose petals curve inwards and create a rounded, ball-like shape.

Indefinite Of a flower which appears at parts of a stem other than the top and so does not terminate the plant.

Also, can be used in reference to parts of a plant or flower which are not easily numbered, because there are so many.

Indehiscent Describes fruit or seeds which do not open to release seeds, for example the fruit of a sweet chestnut (*Castanea sativa*). These kinds of fruits require the outer covering to be removed before attempts at propagation can be made. The opposite is *dehiscent*.

Indentation The zig-zagged edge of a leaf or petal.

Indeterminate When describing an inflorescence, this term means that the flower stems are not terminated by a single flower at the tip but have flowers all the way up the stem. The lower flowers usually open first.

In the context of plants in general, it can mean that the stem will carry on growing indefinitely, as in the case of cordon-grown tomatoes.

Indigenous Originating in the country where it is found; not exotic.

Indumentum This is an all-over covering of hairs which is sometimes found on leaves and stems; the most general term for hair on plants.

Induplicate Folded inwards.

Indurate To harden or to weather; hardened.

Indusiate Possessing an 'indusium'.

Indusium A protective membrane or covering, for example, a larva case.

Inerm Unarmed; also describes a plant having no spikes or thorns.

Infect To taint with disease.

Inferior Situated beneath; lower.

Infertile Having no, or very few nutrients; not fertile, barren, as in soil where nothing grows; or of plants which produce no fruit.

Infest/Infestation To beset in a trouble-some way, as pests do to plants.

Infield Land which is situated near a farmhouse and is constantly manured, tilled and in use.

Inflated Blown up and swollen.

Inflected Bent or flexed.

Inflexed Bent inwards in the direction of the main axis.

Inflorescence Another word for flowers and their arrangement on a stem. Inflorescences vary greatly and have their own individual terms of reference, for example, 'corymb', 'umbel' and 'panicle', which all describe the different shapes the flowers form.

Informal Describes flowers which are irregularly shaped, for example some cultivated varieties of dahlias and chrysanthemums.

The term may also be applied to a garden which is not laid out in strict bedding schemes and contains 'naturalized' plantings and wildflowers.

Infra – A prefix which means below.

Infrageneric Any part of the taxonomical grouping of plants below a 'genus', for example, sub-genus, species and sub-species.

Infraspecific Any part of the taxonomical grouping of plants below that of 'species', for example, 'sub-species', 'variety' and 'cultivar'.

Infructescence The stage at which flowers become fruit.

Infundibular Funnel-shaped.

Inorganic Artificially produced or containing chemicals, as opposed to natural 'organic' substances which are made up of carbon.

Inorganic compounds are common in fertilizers and soil improvers.

Insect Usually small, invertebrate creatures, whose bodies are divided into distinctly recognisable sections.

Insecticide This term refers to a substance used for destroying insects which are considered to be a pest. Insecticides come in many forms: liquid, dust, smoke and so on. Many ready-mixed insecticides are commercially available, meaning that users come into less contact with potentially harmful chemicals.

Insectiverous Plants which trap insects and break down their bodies for food and minerals, particularly nitrogen. Probably the best-known insectiverous plant is *Dionaea muscipula*, the Venus' fly trap.

Also known as 'carnivorous'.

Insert/Insertion The placing of a cutting into a growing medium.

Insignificant Used of flowers which are very small and add no real value to a plant, for example, the small yellow flowers of Alexandrian laurel, *Danae racemosa*.

Integument The two coats which cover the ovule and develop into the seed coat.

Inter A prefix meaning either between or among.

Intercalary Inserted between others.

Intercropping This is the practice of planting fast-growing vegetables between slower-growing crops to ensure the best use of limited space. The fast growers use the space and light before the slower-growing crop has matured enough to actually need them. Examples of vegetables used in intercropping include radishes and lettuces (fast) and parsnips and sweetcorn (slow).

Crops may also be planted in alternate rows or chequer-board style.

Interfoliar Between the leaves, for example, of flowers which appear between the foliage.

Intergeneric Describes a hybrid which is formed between two or more closely related genera. Such a plant is designated with a preceding 'x'. An example of a generic hybrid is x *Cupressocyparis leylandii* (*Cupressus macrocarpa* x *Chamaecyparis nootkatensis*).

Intermediate Describes hybrids which exhibit characteristics of both parents in equal proportion.

Internodal cuttings Pieces of stem cut for 'vegetative' propagation, are taken between nodes.

Internode The part of the stem situated between 'nodes'.

Interrupted Not continuous; said of an arrangement of leaves or petals which would be symmetrical were it not for undeveloped organs, for example.

Interspecific hybrid Hybrid of two different species that are in the same genus. This is indicated by having the generic name followed by an 'x' and then the specific name.

Intra A prefix which means either within or inside.

Intricate Entangled or complex.

Introrse Facing inwards.

Invaginated To be introverted or enclosed in a sheath.

Inverted Upside down.

Involucel A secondary involucre.

Involucre A circle of bracts which overlap. Though found underneath the flowers of plants such as daisies, they are easily seen.

Involute Rolled inwards at the margins.

Irishman's cutting Shoots which develop of their own accord around the base of plants, such as chrysanthemums, and have roots already attached. They can be removed and potted on individually.

Iron An element (chemical symbol Fe) essential for plant health; found naturally in soil.

Irregular Asymmetrical. *Applied to a flower which cannot be divided into equal halves in more than one direction*

Irrigation Any type of watering, for example, with a watering can, hose pipe and especially, automatic systems such as those for lawns and greenhouses.

Island bed A shaped patch of soil or bed for growing plants, usually surrounded by lawns, paths or gravel.

Isobilateral Having alike opposite parts; symmetrical on two planes.

Isomerous Having the same number of parts, in particular, the same number of floral whorls.

J

Jacket The outer covering or skin, particularly of a potato.

Jag/Jagged Used with reference to sharp edged leaves; cleft or division.

Japanese garden A garden designed and laid out in the style of the Japanese, where nature and culture meet in water, stone, statuary and plant life. A place of peace and harmony where one can rest.

The native religion of *Shinto* teaches that places of beauty are where the spirits dwell, so Japanese gardens are mystical, spiritual places.

Jardinière A decorative vessel that is used for growing house plants, or for displaying cut flowers.

Jekyll, Gertrude An influential English garden designer (1843-1932), she studied at the Kensington School of Art and came to gardening late in life, having wanted to become a painter. Instead, she used her artistic eye in planting schemes, being very skilful with colour. She created natural-looking planting schemes using cottage garden plants in drifts.

Gertrude Jekyll worked closely with Edwin Lutyens, a landscape architect whom she worked with on her home at Munstead Wood.

Jellicoe, Geoffrey An English landscape architect and town planner, born in 1900. One of his more famous works is the Caveman Restaurant at Cheddar Gorge, England, designed in 1936.

John Innes compost Sterile loam-based composts for use with pot plants. John Innes is not a trade name but a horticultural institute set up in the early part of the twentieth century for the purposes of research.

John Innes was a property dealer in the city of London, who in 1904 bequeathed his fortune to the improvement of horticulture by experiment and research. The John Innes Horticultural Institute was set up, originally at Merton in Surrey and now at Norwich.

In the 1930s the Institute set out to overcome the problems of unsterilized, unbalanced composts which led to the determining of the physical properties and nutrition required to achieve optimum rates of plant growth, and methods of heat sterilization.

John Innes composts contain: loam, the main body of the compost, including clay which absorbs and releases nutrients; sphagnum moss peat for porosity and aeration and gradually to decompose into humus; sand to condition the soil and improve drainage; fertilizer, nitrogen, phosphates, potash and trace elements.

John Innes is suitable for all but lime-hating plants, and can be recognized by the JIMA (John Innes Manufacturers Association) seal of approval displayed on the packaging.

Joint Also known as a 'node', the point at which a leaf or stem originates.

Jugate Describes a plant which carries leaves opposite each other and in pairs.

Jugum A pair of opposite leaves.

June drop A natural occurrence whereby fruit trees drop fruit before it is ripe during June and July. This prevents the tree from being over-burdened with fruit.

Other causes of June drop are dryness at the roots, weak growth and inept pollination of the blossoms.

Jute The common name and product of two species of corchorus. The product is a fibre used for woven bags, sacks, mats, canvas, etc obtained from the tree bark.

Juvenile The young growth of a plant when it differs from adult growth in appearance of leaves or other aspect. For example, the immature leaves of *Eucalyptus gunnii* are round and blue-green as opposed to the lance-shaped, green adult foliage.

Gardeners may exploit this where juvenile features are thought to be more attractive than those of the adult, by hard pruning annually to promote the flush, young growth.

K

K Chemical symbol for potassium.

Kainite A mineral compound made of hydrous magnesium sulphate with potassium chloride which was once used as a fertilizer in a similar way to potassium today. It is found in salt deposits.

Kaolinite China clay; hydrated aluminium silicate – a particularly flaky kind of clay soil.

Kapok The silky envelope which covers the seeds of the silk-cotton tree, *Ceiba pentandra*, used for stuffing cushions, stuffed toys etc.

Keel The two lower petals of some plants of the *Leguminosae* family, such as sweet peas, which come together in the shape of the keel of a boat.

Keeled Possessing a keel.

Keiki The offshoot of an orchid produced in a node.

Keiki paste A type of hormone used to encourage orchids to produce 'keikis' or 'offshoots'.

Kelp Large brown seaweed which grows below low-tide level. When burnt or rotted it can be used as a fertilizer, yielding potash, iodine and soda.

Kerf A piece of turf or single layer of hay.

Kernel The edible part of a nut seed, encased in a hard outer shell.

Kex The hollow stem of many plants of the *Umbelliferae* family.

Key The seeds of maples and ash which have dry, papery wings to aid their dispersal by wind.

Kidney potato Oval-shaped varieties of potato, such as 'Belle de Fontenay'.

Kidney bed An isolated flower or mixed bed, shaped like a kidney, that is sited in a lawn – an interesting departure from borders or circular beds. Also known as an 'island bed'.

Kinin A plant hormone involved in cell division. Also exploited commercially for drying flowers. *Kinetin*

Kinnikinic A leaf and bark mixture that is made from species of cornel, smoked by native American Indians, rather like tobacco is today.

Kino The resin yielded from the bark of *Pterocaropus* trees, which has astringent properties and used for medicinal purposes.

Kitchen garden A garden that is devoted to the growing of vegetables, fruit and herbs, traditionally walled and solely for the use of the grower themselves as opposed to the market. Flowers might also be incorporated for cutting to avoid disturbing planting schemes in other parts of the garden.

Klendusic Of plants with a built-in protective mechanism which helps them to withstand disease.

Klinostat A revolving platform used in experiments on growing plants.

Knag See knot.

Knar A 'knot' in a tree.

Knee see 'pneumataphore'.

Kneeing The practice of double staking plants, especially sweet peas, with stakes set at some distance apart. Forcing the stem away from one stake a few inches from the ground and then training it up another stake improves flowering, apparently as a result of the restriction of sap.

A similar principle applies with espalier fruit trees, and when branches are held down with weights.

Knife A gardener's essential tool. Various types for different purposes are available: pruning, budding, etc.

Knitch Another name for a faggot.

Knob The remains of the previous year's fruit stalk on a fruit tree, which will produce further fruit buds in the future.

Knock down A reference to the instantaneous effect of some pesticides. Usually implies that they are not long lasting.

Knock out The process of temporarily removing a containerized plant from its pot in order to check the condition of its rootball. This might be done to look for pests, such as vine weevils, or to see whether the plant is pot-bound, in which case the roots will be starting to run circularly around the base of the pot.

Knoll A mound or small hillock.

Knopper gall The symptomatic sticky growths on acorns attacked by gall wasps.

Knosp A flower bud before it has opened.

Knot The thickened part of a tree where the branch is attached to the trunk. A node or joint in a stem, especially that of grass. Also known as a 'knag'.

Knot garden An elaborately-designed, old-fashioned garden of herb and flower beds bordered by low-growing hedges, such as box. Ideally viewed from above to appreciate its intricate patterns.

Knuckle An American term for bud union, the point where the bud and rootstock join.

Knur (Nur) A knotty or balled growth on a tree trunk.

Kumquat Refers to a small and slightly bitter citrus fruit.

Kyanize A method of preserving wood developed in the eighteenth century, named after its inventor, John Kyan.

L

Labellum The petal or petals of flowers of the orchid family which are lip-like in their appearance.

Labels These are made of various materials, and the more you spend the more attractive they will be. They are made from plastic, terracotta, copper, aluminium and so on and are intended to withstand the elements and be large enough to fit all the information you need about the plant. Most are inserted in the ground but some are available with loops to hang them on larger plants at eye level. It is important to label areas that have been planted, particularly when you are sowing seeds and planting bulbs, so that you know, firstly, that something has been planted there and, secondly, what it is so that you can tend it properly. Labelling herbaceous plants is often a good idea, as they die down in winter and might be accidentally dug up.

Labiate A description of lipped flowers/plants; also any member of the plant family, *Labiatae*.

Labium The lower petals of plants which display lipped flowers.

Lace bugs Members of the *Hemiptera* insect group, one species of which, the rhododendron bug, is a pest. Adults and nymphs of *Stephanitis rhododendri* cause discoloration and limp foliage on rhododendrons.

Laced The cut, lacy border of a dianthus flower, usually of a contrasting colour.

Lacecap A type of flower that is exemplified by certain types of hydrangea, which are flat on top and the outer flowers are enlarged and sterile.

Lacerate Of a leaf margin or petal which has an irregularly toothed appearance, as if cut.

Lacewing Members of the *Neuroptera* order of insects whose larvae eat aphids.

Lachrymose Refers to a drooping or pendulous shape which certain plants characteristically assume.

Laciniate Cut-edged, of leaves or petals.

Lacrimiform Tear-shaped.

Lacuna A small hole or depression in a pitted surface, particularly referring to pores or air holes.

Lacunose Full of air holes; pitted.

Ladybird A winged, brightly coloured beetle of the *Coccinellidae* family, often spotted, which is a very welcome predator on aphids and currant mite, as are its young larvae.

Laevigate See levigate.

Lageniform Flask-shaped.
Also refers to a thin plate or layer.

Lamellate Made up of one or more thin plates or scales, laid down in layers.

Lamellicorn A family of once troublesome pests, which includes the cockchafer. Feeders on cereals and root crops.

Lamina The thin, flattened part of a leaf excluding its stem; the leaf blade.

Lanate Woolly and matted.

Lanceolate Shaped like a lance, its widest point in the middle. Usually applied to leaf shapes which are tapered at both ends and two or three times longer than they are broad.

Landscape This term has a number of meanings: it can refer to the natural appearance of an area, normally the part being viewed at the time.
Gardeners take that area and cultivate it and this is known as landscaping. Lancelot 'Capability' Brown was a famous landscaper of the eighteenth century, famed for employing hundreds of workers to move vast tracts of land and create hills and undulating pastures as far as the eye could see.
Garden design can take into account even landscape which is not within its jurisdiction – the area beyond the boundaries of the garden, known as borrowed landscape. Creating a cottage garden, using rolling fields and the heights and scale of distant trees is a way of mutually enhancing both garden and vista.

Lanky A term used on stems which show weak, spindly growth. This might occur where stems have struggled to reach the light and have therefore become elongated, for example.

Lantern cloche An old-fashioned glass cover for protecting a plant from the elements, especially frost.

Lanuginose Covered in short, soft hairs.

Larva/Larvae The immature, pre-pupal stage of moths, flies and butterflies. Also known as grubs and caterpillars, larvae are big eaters and can cause a lot of damage to plants.

Latent Of buds which do not develop unless stimulated in some way, usually by pruning.

Lateral Any sideshoot or branch growing from the main stem.

Latex A milky fluid, such as the sap of rubber trees.

Lath house A building which provides a certain amount of shade as it is roofed with brushwood or slatted wood. It is particularly popular in the hot climate of South America.

Laticiferous Describes any plant which manufactures latex.

Lattice / Latticework Thin strips of metal, plastic or wood placed across each other at right angles with square spaces between to make an open screen. Such screens can be used to grow climbing plants up and are good for breaking up a long garden without the feature being too demanding on the eye.

Lattice pots These are normal plastic pots but with holes in the side to allow roots to penetrate the surrounding soil where the pot is planted. This contains the plant, making it easy to lift and restricting it from spreading.

Bulbs which need to be lifted at the end of the flowering period and marginal water plants which tend to be invasive are often planted out in this way. However, in the case of the aquatic plants, the pot should also be lined with a durable but permeable material, such as hessian for example, so that the soil does not get washed away.

Lawn An expanse of green, kept short for ornamental, practical or, very often, for recreational use. Most commonly this 'green' is actually grass which is regularly mowed and cultivated. It should ideally be flat. Other plants, such as the sweet-smelling chamomile and moss, are also used to cover the ground.

Lawns come in all shapes, sizes and situations, including almost vertical banks, making maintenance a less than simple task. Indeed, apart from mowing from time to time many people leaves lawns to fend for themselves. For a good-quality, attractive-looking lawn, however, it should be fed, watered in dry seasons and aerated in the autumn to encourage root growth and remove thatch.

Lawn rake A fan-shaped rake used to remove moss, thatch and other debris which collects on the surface of lawns.

Lawn sand A sand/chemical mix which is spread on lawns in any but extremely hot weather as part weedkiller/part lawn fertilizer used to kill weeds and moss and improve the quality of the sward.

Lax Usually refers to branches which are not rigid, but loose or floppy.

Laxpendent Hanging loosely.

Layer A plant produced by the practice of layering.

Layering A method of plant propagation which involves burying part of a stem into soil, while still remaining on the parent plant.

It is best to take a fairly fresh shoot and scrape some of the bark from the stem to encourage roots to form in the soil. The stem can be pegged into the soil, halfway down its length so that a few inches of its tip remains above surface. Once the layer has formed its own roots, the shoot can be separated from the parent and you have a whole new plant.

Shrubs, such as rhododendrons, cherry laurel and clematis, respond well to this form of propagation. Border carnations and any plants which send out runners, such as strawberries, also benefit from this type of propagation.

Other types of layering include: air layering whereby the stem is encouraged to root while still being attached to the parent plant.

Leach The removal of soluble substances due to the passage of water through soil. In soils which have very good drainage, such as sandy soils, elements are leached away quite quickly.

Leader The terminal shoot of a plant or central stem.

Leaf A plant organ which is usually flat, emanating from the stems. Leaves contain chlorophyll – the green substance by which they convert sunlight into food for themselves – so are usually green, but they may also be tinged with blue, purple and so on.

Leaves are variable: the spikes of cacti, for example, are leaves which have modified to have as little surface area as possible, meaning least water loss – their spikiness is to protect their swollen stems from predators.

Leaves are appreciated in garden design for their variable shapes, colours, textures and habit (the shape they give the plant). Some designers believe that these characteristics are more important than the flowers, as flowers are fleeting while the leaves can give viewers an all-year round pleasure.

Leaves which change colour in the autumn before falling (on deciduous plants) are especially favoured, having been the source of inspiration to many a poet and writer. Known as 'autumn colour', some plants, such as *Fothergilla major*, the sycamore, beech tree and many more have gorgeous flame colours sometimes being red, yellow and gold on the same plant.

Leafcutter bees Relatives of the honey bees, these are solitary bees which cut pieces out of the leaves of roses and other ornamental plants to make cells in wood and bricks etc. Damage to plants is not severe but it affects the aesthetic value of the foliage.

Leafhoppers A range of sap-consuming insects of the *Hemiptera* group whose plant prey includes rhododendrons, roses, apples, strawberries, raspberries and potatoes. Most do not cause severe damage themselves but some are undesirable because they transmit disease and some cause unattractive leaf mottling.

Leaflet A component part or division of a compound leaf, which looks like a leaf in its entirety.

Lean-to A type of greenhouse which leans against a wall. It should be positioned against a south-facing wall as light is lacking from one whole side. It benefits from deriving heat from the house against which it is positioned.

Leatherjackets The larvae of cranefly or daddy-long-legs (*Tipuladae*). They are pests of cultivated lawns and areas which have previously been pasture. They are brown and up to in 5cm (2in) in length, and cause damage to the roots of plants, especially seedlings. Damage to lawns appears as yellow areas, particularly pronounced in dry weather.

Leathery Soft but thickened; coriaceous.

Leggy Describes the stems of plants which do not receive enough light and so become elongated and drawn in their efforts to reach it.

Legume The seed of members of the family, *Leguminosae*, typically a two-halved pod of the pea or bean.

Lenticel Often seen on the bark of fruit trees, such as prunus, this is a raised breathing pore.

Lenticellate Having lenticels.

Lenticellular Shaped like a lens; a 2-D oval shape, like a lentil.

Lentiginous Minutely dotted or freckled.

Lepidote Also leprous; meaning covered in small scales.

Leprous See lepidote.

Level For easy mowing, lawns should be as level as possible – an important consideration when sowing a lawn or turfing.

Levigate Smooth or polished looking.

Liana A woody climbing vine. Many common house plants, such as umbrella plants (schefflera), are actually lianas which, in the wild, climb up trees from the jungle floor.

Lianoid Like a liana in appearance.

Lichen A fungus and an alga growing symbiotically (to the mutual benefit of one another) to form a pale green crinkly crust on walls, pots, trees, etc. Lichen normally appears in wetter areas where air pollution is low, and on trees whose health is already poor, although it is worth noting that lichen is not thought to cause further damage.

Lifting To remove plants from the soil. This usually refers to the removal of spring bedding, such as wallflowers, to make way for summer bedding, such as busy lizzies, which will continue the flowering display.

Light A reference to soil with a high content of sand and little clay (soil with more clay than sand is, by contrast, known as heavy).

Light Essential for plant growth and health, providing the energy with which plants are able to make growth. House plants, in particular, suffer where light levels are low, symptoms being elongated, straggly growth where stems have struggled to reach light, followed by yellowing of the leaves, leaf drop and eventual death of the plant.

Lights The see-through covers of a cold frame, used in 'hardening off'. Lights are usually left off increasingly during the day to accustom plants to the outdoor climate and returned at night, especially if frosts are threatening.

Lighting Lighting is an excellent way of extending the use of the garden as an out-side room, increasing one's living space. Garden lighting is available in a number of forms, including electric lights – either free-standing or attached to walls, candles and so on.

Lightning An important fixer of nitrogen, returning the gas to the soil for use by plants, but also a potential cause of damage to trees, particularly those planted in isolation. Those trees struck by lightning usually show a loss of bark, often with a gash down one side of the tree. The tree's internal tissues are thereby weakened and thus more vulnerable to disease.

Ligneous Of a woody texture.

Lignose See ligneous.

Lignotuber Some shrubs have a swollen woody base which helps them cope with drought and fire.

Ligulate Having a ligule; like a strap.

Ligule A strap-shaped corolla in plants. Also a scale at the top of a leaf sheath found in grasses and palms.

Limb Branch of a tree.

Lime Calcium compounds; a limey soil is one which contains a high proportion of calcium, making it alkaline. Lime has several gardening applications: it is a plant food, a pH changer (from acid to alkaline or neutral) and it also improves soil texture by breaking up clay soils.

Lime is available in a number of different forms – mushroom compost, chalk, limestone, calcium carbonate, quicklime (calcium oxide) and hydrated or slaked lime (calcium hydroxide).

Lime has many horticultural uses: it may be added to an excessively acid soil to facilitate the growing of plants which do not tolerate high levels of calcium in soils, although it is probably best to grow plants which would naturally grow there. Similarly the addition of lime to acid compost allows micro-organisms therein to decompose matter more efficiently.

While lime is useful for the above applications, an excess of lime is potentially damaging; it can lock up iron in the soil causing lime-induced chlorosis to plants; it can also destroy humus and waste nitrogen.

Lime-dots See hydathode.

Linnaeus, Carl von Linne A Swedish botanist (1707-1778) who devised the system of binomial nomenclature which provides the basis for the classification of plants still in use today. He ordered plants taxonomically by classifying them according to their flower parts (sexual characteristics).

Line out Placing cuttings or seedling plants in lines in a nursery bed or greenhouse.

Linear To have parallel margins
    Can also mean elongated.

Liner A pliable plastic sheeting made of PVC (polyvinyl chloride) or butyl rubber used to line the bottom and sides of a pond. All are flexible and fit the shape of a pond easily.

Lingulate Like a tongue.

Lip The petals of some flowers are described as lips. For example, those of the *Labiatae*, such as the flowers of lamium (dead nettle), which have a hooded upper petal and lower petal on which pollinators can land.

Lithomorphic One of the ten major soil groups in the system of Avery *et al*. Lithomorphic soils tend to be shallow and drought-prone.

Lithophyte A plant which grows on rock or stony ground, obtaining water and nutrients from the air.

Littoral Inhabiting the seashore.

Liquid manure This term originated from the liquid which drained from the stable floor; nowadays it can mean anything from the liquid that results from the placing of dung in water to soluble chemical fertilizers.

Loam This term is used to refer to soil in general, but also to the archetypal soil which is the best medium in which to grow plants. This is a balance of clay, sand and organic matter.

Lobe A rounded segment, usually of a leaf division.

Lobed Having rounded segments.

Lobulate Having lobules.

Lobule A small lobe.

Locular Also *loculate,* having locules. *divided into chambers*

loculus/
Locule Small cavities or chambers, for example, those found in fruit.

Loculicidal Dehiscing (splitting) along the back of the carpel.

Lodicule A small scale of grass flower.

Lomentum A pod of the *Leguminosae* family which breaks into pieces at constrictions between the seeds.

Lorate Strap-shaped.

Lunate(d) Crescent-shaped.

Lute/Luting An implement, made out of a long piece of wood, for working a top-dressing evenly into a lawn. It is especially useful for working in topdressing where a large area has to be covered.

Lyrate Lyre-shaped; having a larger terminal lobe than the lateral ones.

M

Macrobiotic Refers to seeds which will germinate after a long period of dormancy, given the right conditions.

Macropore A large pore in soil; the space which is found between soil particles. Macropores are found in soils which are made up of larger particles, for example, those with a high sand content.

Macrospore A large spore, that is also a known as megaspore.

Maculate Describes a leaf or flower that has speckled or spotted markings.

Maggot A general term covering the larvae of flies.

Magnesium An element essential for the manufacture of chlorophyll in plants. A magnesium deficiency shows as a yellowing between the leaf veins of the older leaves as the element is given first to the younger leaves.

Maiden A tree in its first year after having been grafted onto a rootstock.

Maincrop A term used to cover both the largest crop which a plant produces in a cropping season and the variety which produces it.

Maintenance pruning A process of gradual pruning, whereby dead, diseased and other unproductive stems are removed from fruit trees. This encourages new growth and hence better fruiting.

Malic acid An acid contained in the cells of fruit, such as apples.

Mallee A small type of eucalyptus tree which, having adapted to fire or drought, has swollen stems at its base.

Mamillate Nipple-shaped.

Manganese One of the trace elements which plants require, but only in very small amounts.

Manure A general term for bulky, organic material which improves the soil consistency and increases its nutrient content. For example, horse manure is a traditional soil improver, as are leafmould, garden compost, spent hops, mushroom-compost and green manure, a planted crop such as clover which is ploughed into the soil while still young.

Manures are fertilizers, although in gardening terms the word 'manure' tends to be applied to organic, bulky nutrients while 'fertilizers' tend to be inorganic and come in more concentrated forms, such as bonemeal.

Manure is used to enrich the soil over a long period of time as it takes such a length of time to be broken down by soil organisms.

Manure fork A multi-tined fork with a long handle, which is used specifically to handle manure.

Marbled A description used of leaves or flowers which are mottled like marble.

Marcescent Leaves which remain on the plant after they have died are described thus. This characteristic is used to good effect in beech (fagus) hedging, whereby the autumn leaves turn an attractive brown, persist all through the winter, maintaining the hedge's efficiency as a screen and then drop when the new growth appears.

Margin The outer edge of leaves, usually referred to only if of significance, for example, if variegated or crinkled.

Marginal A plant which grows in the water margins, where its roots are partially submerged, for example, *Iris pseudacorus*, the common flag iris.

Maritime climate The mild weather (lacking extremes of drought and frost) enjoyed in coastal areas.

Marl/Marlite This refers to a fertilizer that is made from granulated clay with a high lime content.

Marsh A waterlogged area which never drains, often low-lying, supporting particular types of plants and wildlife; also known as a 'fen'.

Mat Dead grass and other organic matter in lawns and grass which forms a suffocating layer on the surface of the soil. Mat can be removed by regular scarifying or raking.

Maturate To encourage something to mature; to become completely ripe.

Mature Fully developed.

Maze An old-fashioned, labyrinth-like area of a garden, a kind of play area in which tall hedges, winding paths and dead-ends obscure the exit. The whole landscape forms a geometric shape which can be appreciated from above.

Meadow/Water meadow A field of grass used for making hay. Low-lying meadows near rivers and streams, which are frequently waterlogged, are known as water meadows.

Mealy Powdery.

Mealy bug A house and greenhouse pest which congregates on stems and sucks out plant sap. It is segmented like a wood-louse and is covered in a fluffy-looking, waxy substance.

Mealy bug should be wiped off the plant and dabbed with white spirit on the end of a paintbrush. Systemic insecticides containing dimethoate can also be used.

Mechanical injury Damage which is caused to plants by physical mishandling, for example, accidentally cutting a tree with a lawnmower or trapping the leaves of a house plant in a drawer.

Median Relates to the central transverse area of a leaf.

Medium A term which describes a soil which is balanced – not too heavy with clay, not too light with sand, but of medium consistency, the best loam for growing.

   Official agricultural bodies have defined this texture as a soil with less than two-thirds of the sand being between 0.06-0.2mm and less than one-third is larger than 0.6mm.

Medullary Consisting of or resembling pith; spongy.

Megasporangium Producing macro- or megaspores.

Megaspore See macrospore.

Megasporophyll The carpel of flowering plants; in non-flowering plants, the sporophyll bearing megaspores.

Membrane A thin, flexible sheet, usually translucent, such as a cell covering.

Membraneous Like a membrane.

Mentum A chin-like protuberance of some flowers, for example, some orchids.

Mericarp A one-seeded carpel which is one of a pair split at maturity.

Meristem The formative tissue of plants, having the power of cell division. Meristem cells cause growth in plants.

Meristem culture The use of meristems in propagation.
   Also known as micropropagation

Meristematic cell The area of growth division found in plants.

Mesochile The middle of the three part lips of some orchid flowers.

Mesophyte Plants which live on land and require water when in growth, intermediate between a xerophyte (plants which live in drought conditions) and a hydrophyte (plants which live in water).

Mesosperm The middle coat of a seed.

Metabolism Chemical changes in living organisms, including processes inherent to life, such as photosynthesis.

Metaldehyde A chemical used in pellet form to kill slugs and snails. It is 'unfriendly' because it is non-specific, meaning that it is also poisonous to birds and pets. It is generally thought better to use an alternative control, such as pellets containing aluminium sulphate which do not harm birds and other wildlife, or a 'biological control'.

Methylated spirit An alcohol-based fluid used in pest control, for example, of mealy bugs.

Microclimate A localized area of a certain temperature and climate. For example, the south-west of Ireland has a very mild, moist microclimate which supports a range of tender plants. Other environments which can be described as microclimates include heated greenhouses and bottle gardens.

Micro-organism Any living thing which is too small to be seen by the naked eye, such as an amoeba or a bacterium.

Microbe Another term for micro-organism.

Micronutrient A trace element which is needed in only very small amounts for plant health.

Microphyllous Describes plants which have very small leaves.

Microphyte A tiny plant.

Micropore A small pore space found in soil. The size of the spaces between soil particles is defined by the size of the soil particles themselves; the smaller the soil particles, the less space between them. Micropores therefore tend to be found in soils with a predominance of clay.

Micropropagation The practice of raising plants from tissue culture. Isolated parts of the plant are grown under glass and their conditions of food, light and temperature are closely regulated.

Micropylar Relating to a micropyle.

Micropyle An orifice in the ovule coating, through which the pollen tube enters.

Microspore The smaller of two forms of spore; a spore which develops into a male gametophyte.

Midrib The main vein which runs down the middle of a leaf.

Midvein See midrib.

Mildew A fungus which occurs on plants, giving them a dusty, white appearance. Associated with both very dry and damp conditions, common mildews are powdery mildew and downy mildew.

Millepede A root-eating arthropod which lives in soil and leaf debris. It has many legs and is segmented, but differs from centipedes in having one pair of legs per segment rather than two. Although millepedes usually feed on rotting plants, they can affect roots and seedlings, most often in spring and particularly those which have already been attacked by other pests.

Mimic Any plant which resembles another plant or thing. For example, lithops are called 'living stones' because of their likeness to pebbles.

Mimosiform Having flowers like those of mimosa, with showy stamens and an inconspicuous calyx and corolla, making the flowers appear like balls of fluff.

Mineral Neither animal nor vegetable; minerals include elements and rocks.

Mist propagation A means of propagating plants via rooted cuttings, either in an open greenhouse or in a closed unit, such as a propagator. Both create a warm, damp environment by incorporating a soil-heating element or cables, a thermostat and misting nozzle heads set to a timer switch so that cuttings are sprayed at regular intervals.

The process causes cuttings to root much more quickly because moisture and heat loss is reduced and the risk of fungal diseases is literally washed away by the misters.

Mite Members of the *Arachnaceae*, more commonly known to us as spiders. They are differentiated from insects by having four pairs of legs (instead of three) and also by having no division between their head, thorax and abdomen. In the greenhouse, a frequent example is the red spider mite which thrives in hot, dry conditions and unfortunately infests tomatoes, cucumbers, carnations and fuchsias among others.

Mitosis Describes a sequence of cellular changes which takes place in reproduction, whereby cells divide in four elaborate phases.

Mock trenching More commonly known as 'double digging', whereby soil is cultivated to two spade spits depth – about 60cm (2ft) without bringing the less fertile subsoil to the top. Ground which has been uncultivated for a long time and has been compacted, or where deep-rooting plants are to be planted will benefit from this practice.

Moder humus Organic matter which is partially broken down and slightly incorporated into the soil.

Monadelphus Stamens whose filaments are fused into a single group.

Moniliform Describes any organ which, being constricted at intervals along its length, appears like a string of beads or knotted rope.

Mono A prefix meaning one.

Monocarpellary Of a fruit which is derived from one carpel.

Monocarpic Refers to plants that flower only once, after fruiting.

Monocotyledon Having one seed leaf (as opposed to a dicotyledon, having two). Leaves have parallel veins, petals are in threes and the plant has no cambium. For example grasses and sedges. *abb. monocot*

Monocephalous Possessing one flower head only.

Monochlamydeous Having one perianth whorl only.

Monocot The flowering plant world is divided into monocots and dicots, in other words, plants which possess one cotyledon in their seed and those which have two. Examples of monocots include grasses, lilies, orchids, irises and bromeliads.

Monocotyledonous Containing only one cotyledon in the seed.

Monoculture The practice of growing only one crop in a large area, such as large amounts of maize in fields.

Monoecious Carrying bisexual flowers on the same plant, as opposed to 'dioecious' which carry male and female flowers on the same plant.

Monoembryonic Ovules or seeds which carry one embryo.

Monogeneric Of a plant family which contains only one genus.

Monopetalous Having only one petal.

Monopodial A stem which has no sideshoots or laterals.

Monospecific See monotypic.

Monotypic Applied to families or genera with only one member.

Moisture meter This term describes a meter which gauges the amount of moisture that is to be found in the soil. It is used for the propagation of cuttings and containerized plants – usually within a commercial context.

Mole Considered to be a garden pest due to the molehills (piles of earth) they create in lawns, moles burrow under the ground feeding on soil organisms, such as worms. While they do not feed on plants directly they cause damage by the uprooting effects which are most present in winter and spring.

There are a number of ways of deterring moles from the garden; placing traps in the soil, poison which must be administered by an expert, or employ a mole catcher. Deterrents are also available which try to repulse moles with smokes, smells or vibrations.

Montmorillonite A type of clay present in soil. The soil in which it is found is made up of large soil particles of 1-2 layers of alumino-silicate sheets. This type of soil has a great capacity for water and is therefore very 'plastic'.

Morhumus Organic matter which is found on acid soil. It is not incorporated and remains on the surface of the soil.

Morphology The study of plant structure.

Mortar Mix of cement, sand and water.

Moss pole Also known as a totem pole, this is a plastic or wooden pole covered in sphagnum moss for growing climbing or trailing plants up. It can be kept moist to provide humidity while also providing an attractive, natural-looking support for the plant.

Mother plant The parent of a propagule or the provider of the seed of a hybrid.

Motile Able to move; for example, hairs and self-propelling spores.

Mottles Discoloration of leaves caused by viruses, appearing as rounded yellow areas on the upper surfaces of foliage.

Mottling Soil which is mottled blue on the surface is stagnant as a result of waterlogging. This often occurs on heavy clay soils and is due to anaerobic conditions, which means that soil organisms can no longer survive there.

Mound layering A form of propagation, particularly used on fruit, whereby over a number of years rooted layers are produced. In essence, the process involves cutting back a mother plant early in the growing season to a couple of inches above the ground and placing soil over the top. From this a number of shoots form and roots grow into the soil. These can be removed and then grown on as separate plants. The mother plant can continue to produce further plants by the same process.

Mucilage A viscous material.

Mucronate Describes the abrupt ending of a leaf by the growth of a spur or spine.

Multifid Having many lobes.

Multifoliate Possessing many leaves.

Multigeneric Of hybrids that have many genera as their parents.

Mulch A layer put on the soil for the purposes of moisture retention, weed suppression, fruit protection, soil warming and aesthetic reasons. The layer may be bark chippings, compost, leafmould, straw and even plastic.

Mulches are traditionally applied to the soil in spring when the soil is warming up and contains plenty of moisture. Mulches should not be applied to dry soils as they will remain dry, the mulch preventing water from entering.

Mull Humus which forms under alkaline conditions. It is intimately incorporated into the soil and well broken down. It is therefore attached to the surface of sand grains and joins clay particles together in brown earth.

Multi-dibber A board of dibbers, a time-saving device for making numerous holes for pricking out and striking cuttings at one time.

Multiple fruit A single fruit borne of a number of flowers.

Muriate of potash A plant food made of potassium chloride. Because of its chlorine content, muriate of potash can scorch the leaves of some plants, such as strawberries and tomatoes. It is, however, held in the soil well so can be applied where susceptible plants are not in danger.

Muricate Warty or rough, with projecting sharp points.

Muriculate Slightly muricate.

Muscariform Broom-shaped.

Mushroom compost The waste from spent mushroom beds. It is both a soil improver and a plant food as it usefully contains nitrogen, phosphates, potash and some trace elements. It can be used both as a mulch to suppress weeds and preserve moisture in the soil, or can be dug into the soil.

Mutant A plant or section of a plant which is genetically different from the rest of it. Also called 'sports' by gardeners and breeders who can exploit these natural occurrences and cultivate them to create new plants.

Mycology The study of fungi.

Mycorrhiza(e) Fungus which attaches itself to plant roots and forms a symbiotic relationship (one of mutual benefit) with the plant. This works by the plant giving up sugar to the fungus (albeit reluctantly) while the fungus absorbs phosphates and nitrates from the soil.

It is also thought that mycorrhizae helps plants by fighting off disease and by also producing vitamins that are beneficial to the plants.

Myrmecophyte A plant which has a symbiotic relationship with ants, for example, the jade vine, *Strongylodon macrobotrys*.

N

Nana From the Greek, *nanos*, meaning dwarf, this term is often incorporated as part of plant name, for example, *Berberis thunbergii* 'Nana'.

Nap A lawn surface, especially one which is flattened to lie in one direction; exploited by mowers which press the grass down in the direction in which the mower is going, giving the formal, neat appearance of stripes that lasts for a few days afterwards.

National Growmore A balanced fertilizer made up of nitrogen, phosphoros and potassium in a standard formula.

Native Indigenous; of a plant which occurs naturally in a country or place, as opposed to having been introduced from another environment.

Naturalize To establish plants in their natural environment and in a manner in which they would naturally grow. For example, daffodil bulbs planted in drifts, at random in a lawn or meadow gives the appearance that they have increased themselves as they would do naturally.

It is important to choose plants carefully as cultivated varieties may look artificial: choose native species where possible. However, plants must also be robust in order to withstand competition for food and water from surrounding turf.

Good plants for naturalizing include daffodils, crocus, bluebells, snake's head fritillary and snowdrops.

To give the appearance of naturalizing, sites for planting are chosen and then the bulbs scattered around and planted in groups where they land, as opposed to formal bedding schemes. The soil beneath the turf should be improved by breaking it up and incorporating some compost before planting. Then the lawn should be fed annually with a balanced fertilizer and sulphate of potash to ensure good flowering.

Naturalized Term used of a plant which, having been introduced from another environment, establishes itself in the wild as if native.

Navicular In the shape of the boat with a deep keel, usually referring to the bracts and flowers of grasses.

Neck The point at which growth appears from a bulb, at which the bulb swells.

Neck rot Also known as collar rot, this is fungal decay which appears at the neck of bulbs or the base of plants.

Necrosis This term refers to the death of plant tissue. A part of a plant which had died would be described as having 'necrotic spots'.

Nectariferous Having nectaries.

Nectar Sugary substance produced by plant glands to attract birds and insects to pollinate their flowers. Plant nectaries are situated at the base of the flower so that, in their attempts to reach the nectar, bees etc brush pollen on themselves which is then transferred to the female parts of that plant, or others, the insects visit later.

Nectary A gland in a flower part which secretes nectar.

Needle The leaf of a pine tree or other conifer, which is very thin and covered in a thick waxy coat making it able to withstand harsh weather.

Nematicide Chemical substance used for destroying nematodes.

Nematode A tiny worm, no bigger than 2mm (1/10in) long, found in soils, water and animals which feed on plant tissues. Common examples include the stem eelworm and chrysanthemum eelworm.

Apart from their plant–damaging effects, nematodes have recently had their parasitic habits exploited by gardeners for the purposes of biological control of slugs. *Phasmarhabditis hermaphrodita* enter through a pore in the slug's mantle, releases bacteria and multiplies. In a couple of days the slug stops feeding, burrows down into the soil and shortly dies.

Nerve A midrib or vein of a leaf.

Nerved Having veins and ribs. Also nervose.

Netting A meshed material of nylon, plastic, twine or cotton used around the garden for a number if purposes, including protecting fruit from birds and plants from animals; providing a wind break; providing shade for greenhouses; protecting plants from frost.

Netting films Used as 'floating mulches' to cover young plants, providing protection from the weather and from pests, while raising the under cover temperature to promote growth.

Net virus Virus causing a netting effect on the leaf due to restriction of the veins.

Neuter A flower which, having no sexual organs, is sterile. This is often the case in hybrid flowers where sexual organs have been modified by breeding to become petals, giving double flowers.

Neutral pH 7 The point at which soil is neither acid nor alkaline.

Nicking If a small cut is made in the bark of a tree into the cambium layer, just below a bud, its growth will be inhibited; if one is made above it the bud will be stimulated into growth. Nicking can be used in shaping a tree.

Nicotine A pesticide used for killing aphids in particular. It is often used as a smoke in greenhouses and is extremely toxic to humans as well as insects.

Nigrescent Turning black.

Nip The terminal growth of a plant is nipped or pinched out to promote growth in the sideshoots. This encourages a young plant to become bushy rather than elongated: it is part of the shaping process of plants like fuchsias, for example.

Nip can also be used to describe the effects of frost. Slightly blackened tips are the symptoms of 'nipped' leaves.

Nitrate of lime A granular fertilizer containing nitrogen and lime, making it a good fertilizer for acid soil. Used as a topdressing, it feeds, corrects pH imbalance and accelerates humus composition in the soil.

Nitrate of potash Also known as saltpetre, this is a fertilizer containing nitrogen and potash and can be applied either as a dry powder or a liquid manure.

Nitrate of soda A quick-acting nitrogen fertilizer which is best used in spring and summer. Leaves can be scorched if it is not applied carefully.

Nitro-chalk A proprietary fertilizer that is made up of calcium carbonate and ammonium nitrate, and is used to compensate for a nitrogen deficiency in the soil. Signs of such a deficiency are pale green leaves in plants – perhaps tinged with pink – and reduced vigour.

It is especially useful for acid soils in spring and early summer. Because it tends to attract moisture it should be stored carefully in a dry place.

Nitrogen A chemical element which is an essential plant nutrient, especially important for the development of healthy leaves. Its chemical symbol is N.

Symptoms of nitrogen deficiency include the green disappearing from leaves and the plant looking generally unhealthy – it will also be much smaller than one receiving nitrogen. Methods of rectifying a nitrogen deficiency include the addition made to the soil of nitrogen-containing fertilizers, such as sulphate of ammonia, dried blood and nitrochalk. Balanced fertilizers have equal amounts of nitrogen, potash and phosphate.

No-dig system An organic-gardening practice of not cultivating soil or only very lightly with a trowel rather than a spade, because of a belief that digging encourages weeds, breaks down the soil structure and increases the loss of soil nutrients.

The no-dig system uses mulches instead, planting close to the surface wherever possible.

No-soil composts The use of alternative planting mediums to soil, especially in pot culture. Most often the medium is peat, having the advantages of good aeration and a high porosity.

Because peat is a slow-renewing resource, the reserves of which have been severely depleted in the last decade, peat alternatives are now also in use, for example, coconut fibre or coir.

Nocturnal Of plants and animals which come to life at night. For example, slugs and snails do most damage at night, hiding in foliage and garden debris during the day, while the short-lived flowers of cactus, *Hylocereus undatus*, open at night.

Nodation Knottiness; a knotty place.

Node Where a leaf/leaves, or bud, is attached to a stem. Also called a leaf joint.

Nodous/Nodose Knotty.

Nodular/Nodulose/Noduled/Nodulous Of or like a nodule; having nodules.

Nodule Small knots or swellings found on roots of leguminous plants (*Leguminosae*) which contain bacteria that can trap nitrogen in the air and make it available in the form of ammonia to that plant and those plants grown in the soil thereafter.

This is a symbiotic relationship whereby both the bacteria and plant benefit: the plant receives essential nutrients and the bacteria receive carbohydrate in return.

Nog The stump or snag left on a tree after a portion of it has been removed.

Nomenclature The botanical naming and classification of plants.

Non-resupinate Term used off a flower which has an upside-down appearance by virtue of having a twisted petiole, as is true of some orchids.

Nonvascular Plants which have no vascular tissue, in other words without the xylem and phloem cells which conduct food and water around the plant. These are more primitive plants, such as fungi and algae.

Notch A nick. The incision made above or below buds of apple and other trees, to stimulate or discourage growth, for the purposes of shaping the tree.

Novirame The second year flowering or fruiting shoot of a primocane.

NPK The chemical symbols representing nitrogen, phosphorus and potassium respectively, for a fertiliser which contains elements in equal proportion and is used for all-round plant health. Nitrogen encourages foliage health;

phosphorus root health; and potassium flowers and fruit.

Nucellar From the nucellus.

Nucellus The mass of tissue inside the ovule. In some species of plant the size of the nucellus is used diagnostically to decide which species it is.

Nuciferous Nut-bearing, used of plants which form nuts.

Nuciform In the shape of a nut or like a nut in appearance.

Nuclear stock Plants which are reproduced from cuttings as opposed to seed, from plants which are known to be free of disease.

Nucleus The essential organelle of a cell, which hold the gene-containing chromosomes, controlling the reproduction of cells.
    Can also refer to a small, young bulb of garlic.

Nursery bed An area of soil where seeds and seedlings are raised in the ground and in pots and containers, having already been hardened off but prior to being transferred over to their permanent growing positions. In essence, this area must always be kept moist so plants can take up water, be well drained and sheltered.

Usually outdoors, nursery beds can be of any size and should be enclosed by wooden slatting a few inches high. A layer of permeable fabric may be laid down underneath the pots which serves the purpose of suppressing weeds and soil-borne diseases while allowing the plants to draw water from the soil and drain off into it.

Another method is a sand bed; this involves laying a piece of plastic over the soil and filling the area with coarse sand to the height of the wooden slatting. Then the pots are placed on the surface: the sand holds water meaning that beds need less watering, while allowing excellent drainage.

Nut A dry, woody fruit that is contained in a covering which is indehiscent (not freely opening).

Nutant Of a flower or stem.
    Can also mean nodding.

Nutlet A small nut.

Nymph This term refers to the stage of development of young aphids and certain other insects at which they are mobile, but are without wings, and usually of a different colour.

O

Ob – A prefix meaning 'inverted'.

Obcompressed Flattened from the front to the back.

Obconic Like a cone with the point of attachment at the narrower end.

Obcordate Inversely heart-shaped, of a plant leaf.

Obcuneate The opposite of cuneate or wedge-shaped, so that the greatest width of the leaf is near the stalk

Obelisk A needle-shaped, four-sided monument made of stone, an ornament often employed as a memorial.

Obhastate Arrow-shaped, with the lobes uppermost.

Oblanceolate Of a leaf; like a lance-head but in reverse.

Oblate Spheroid or shaped like an orange but flattened at the top and bottom.

Obligate Essential.

Obligate parasite A parasite which depends solely on its host for its life, for example Mistletoe (*Viscum album*).

Oblique Slanting. Also, of a leaf shape having asymmetrical sides such as the leaves of *Begonia rex*.

Oblong Describes a leaf shape which is between two and four times as long as it is wide.

Oblong-orbiculate Of a leaf shape, which being almost as wide as it is long, appears practically round.

Oblong-ovate An oblong leaf shape with inward curving tips.

Obovate Of a leaf oval in shape with the greatest width furthest from the stalk, like an upside-down egg.

Obovoid Of leaves, petals and fruits which are oval in shape.

Obpyriform Of fruit or leaves which are pear shaped, the stem being attached at the narrowest end.

Obpyrimidal An upside down pyramid.

Obsolescent Going out of use, in the course of disappearing.
bovate reverse of ovate

Obsolete Extinct.
     Also where organs that are usually present are absent.

Obtruncated With top or head removed.

Obtuse Describes a blunt-tipped leaf or petal.

Obverse Describes any leaf whose base is narrower than its tip.

Occluded Meaning completely shut in or closed – this term applies to wounds on trees which have become completely calloused over.

Ocrea A sheath which is made of two stiplules united around a stem.

Odorous Emitting a (usually pleasant) smell; also used are odoriferous and odorant, meaning fragrant.

Oedema Also known as dropsy, this is a condition which causes leaves and stems to develop wart-like growths and is due to over-watering and excessive humidity. Consequently, it is most common on plants grown under glass, some examples being tomatoes, pelargoniums, peppers and begonias.

Officinal Applied to plants which have medicinal properties, therefore it is a frequently used name for the species of many herbs. For example, *Calendula officinalis* (common marigold) and *Rosmarinus officinalis* (rosemary).

Offset A young plant reproduced asexually by the parent, usually at the base. Some bulbs and cacti reproduce in this manner.

Offsets can be removed from the parent, and then potted up and grown on as separate plants.

Offshoot Another word for offset.

Oleaginous Oily.

Olibanum A gum resin which flows from cuts in species of boswellia, commonly called frankincense.

Oligocarpous Bearing little fruit.

Oligotrophic Low nutrient levels; deficient in minerals, but usually high in levels of oxygen. The term can be applied to soil, ponds etc.

Olitory Dated term for a kitchen garden; a pot herb.

Ombrophile Plant which can tolerate a lot of rain; adjective is ombrophilous.

Ombrophobe Plant which is intolerant of a lot of rain; adjective is ombrophobous.

Onion fly *Delia antiqua* is a fly whose maggots feed on the stems and bulbs of onions, shallots and leeks, causing most damage during mid-summer. Two to three generations may actually appear in one growing season.

Soil should be cultivated during winter to get rid of the overwintering pupae; other preventative measures include soil sterilization and dusting seedlings with an insecticide.

Onion hoe A small hand-held hoe with an arched handle leading to a semi-circular blade. It is used for weeding, mainly below thick foliage and, most obviously, onions.

Open-centre The practice of pruning trees to leave the centre free of growth; particularly used on fruit trees.

Operculate Having a operculum.
    Also opercular.

Operculum A cover or lid.

Open ground An area of cultivation out in the open, not covered.

Open soil Another way of describing a 'light' soil, this is one which has a high proportion of sand particles, and therefore has larger pore spaces between particles.
    The larger pores means that the soil contains a greater quantity of air, making it physically lighter to work.

Open pollination This is the type of pollination which occurs naturally between plants and without any assistance from humans.

Oporice A medicine made from quinces and pomegranates.

Opposite Describes a pair of leaves which are positioned on either side of a stem.

Orangery A heated building, usually of three sides, glass on the south side with the north side attached to a house, for the growing of citrus fruit in cool climates. Popular in the last two centuries.

Orbicular A term which means approximately spherical or round.

Orchard An enclosed garden of fruit trees.

Orchard house A glass house for cultivating fruits without using artificial heat.

Ordure Dung or dirt.

Organ A part of a plant which serves a specific purpose.

Organic Strictly, this means anything which contains carbon.

Organic gardening Cultivation without the aid of artificial chemicals.

This is an increasingly popular method of gardening due to fears that pesticides actually do harm by upsetting the natural balance – killing off one pest means that its prey breeds unhindered and then it, too, can become a real problem.

Insects are also known to build up a resistance to chemicals, meaning that increasingly powerful substances have to be used, leaving residues in soil. The insect corpses are eaten by wildlife and can cause harm to humans and animals.

Organic gardening favours growing wild plants which would occur naturally in that environment, rather than battling against nature by trying to raise something that would be happier elsewhere.

Organic matter Plant material, usually decomposing, used as mulches and composts for the purposes of improving the condition of the soil. Examples include mushroom compost, leafmould, bark chippings and manure.

Organic matter may be added to excessively clayey soils, for example, to enhance the drainage and improve soil porosity; similarly, a sandy soil benefits from the addition of organic matter because of improved water retention. Matter in the soil means that the plant roots are able to provide better anchorage for the plant.

Ornamental Plants which are valued for their decorative qualities are described thus. Vegetables grown for their aesthetic rather than practical value, such as ornamental cabbage which is used as winter bedding and in window boxes.

Osseous Bony and brittle.

Orthotropism Growth in the direct line of stimulus, particularly gravity.

Osier Any willow whose branches are used for making baskets, particularly *Salix viminalis*.

Osier bed A patch of soil where osiers (salix) grow.

Osmocote A proprietary controlled-release fertilizer contained in a coated pellet. The fertilizer slowly diffuses into the soil in which it is placed over a period of time.

It is used predominantly for house plants and hanging baskets during the growing season to save the bother of remembering to feed plants on a regular weekly basis. Plants in containers need regular feeding as there is a limited amount of food in the compost, plus the fact that although regular watering is needed, it means nutrients are washed away when the water drains out.

Osmosis The movement of a liquid across a membrane. In this way nutrients and water are transported around plants. Osmotic pressure gives cells turgor, enabling stomatal pores to open and close for the purposes of respiration.

Osmunda fibre A now obsolete constituent of potting compost derived from the dried roots of *Osmunda regalis*, the regal fern. Bark and peat have pretty much taken its place.

Outgrowth An offshoot, sideshoot, or a mutant shoot.

Ovary The female part of a plant contained in the flower. The ovary holds the ovules which, once fertilized, develop into seeds.

Ovate Describes a leaf which is oval but wider near the stalk.

Ovate-acuminate An ovate leaf which has a point at its tip, such as that of *Lunaria annua* (honesty).

Ovate-cordate Of an ovate leaf which has a heart-shaped base.

Over/gone Describes plants which have finished their flowering period, or the flowers themselves.

Overblown Describes a flower that has gone past its best.

Overdressed Petals which have been prepared for show by being bent backwards to the extent that the flower appears unnatural.

Overwinter To keep a plant from autumn through winter. Plants which are susceptible to the action of frost on their leaves and stems are known as tender or semi-tender.

Semi-tender plants which die down in the winter may survive outdoors if their crowns are covered with bracken, peat or straw. Tender plants are overwintered by bringing them indoors, under glass, for the duration of the frosts.

Oviform In the shape of an egg.

Ovoid Of 3-D objects which are shaped like an egg.

Ovule Situated in the ovary, the ovule develops into the seed on fertilization.

Ovulate Having ovules.

Own root A plant which is growing on its own roots, as opposed to those which have been grafted onto a rootstock.

Oxalic Applied to an acid derived from oxalis, wood sorrel, and other plants, which is used as a bleaching agent and for cleaning metals.

Oxygen A gas without smell, taste or colour essential to animal and plant life.

Oxygenator An plant which grows submerged in water and releases oxygen. Also called water weeds, these plants are necessary to keep ponds clear of algae and keep the water alive.

A common example of an oxygenator is Canadian pondweed (*Elodea canadenis*). Considered by some to be an invasive plant, it certainly serves large plants well and if it does start to take over, can be pulled out by the handful quite easily. *Myriophyllum*, water milfoil, is ideal for smaller ponds and has the added benefit of providing shelter and egg-laying sites for pond life.

Oyster The ground shells of oysters were once used as a slow-release calcium fertilizer and were valued because of their porous qualities.

P

Pachycarpous Having a thick pericarp (wall of a fruit).

Painting The practice of painting tree wounds with a special sealant after pruning to reduce the risk of disease. These days it is a controversial practice, as research has shown that painting wounds does not make any real difference. It is more important to prune properly, using the correct equipment and making the cut where the tree will naturally be able to callous over. Pruning of this sort should take place when the tree is not at risk from disease.

Paired Where leaves or shoots appear opposite each other, in pairs, on a stem.

Palea A small, dry scale of a fern leaf or a bract on a grass flower.

Paleaceous Scaly; bearing small, and chaffy bracts.

Palmate A leaf shape with a number of divided lobes, resembling the palm of a hand with the fingers spread, like the leaves of acers.

Palmatifid Of a leaf shape which is shaped like a hand but with the leaf divisions stopping half-way down the 'fingers'.

Palmatisect Palmately cut (not cleft or lobed) into leaf divisions,

Pan

a shallow, round container or pot

Pan (Panning) Also known as a cap, a pan is a layer of hard soil, occurring either on or under the earth surface, and is impermeable to water and oxygen. A pan or cap on the surface of the soil may be caused by by constant traffic over an area, such as the wear sustained by a path. In the soil, pans occur where earth is cultivated continually to a certain point and no deeper, for example, in ploughing.

Roots cannot penetrate pans and seedlings cannot break through pans on the soil surface, so they should be broken up by by hoeing or digging. Pans also occur naturally on heavy clay and iron soils.

Also, a shallow dish for raising seedlings and shallow-rooted plants.

Pandurate(d) Shaped like a violin, with both ends double-lobed (one larger than the other) and narrowing in the middle. Also panduiform.

Panicle Branching indeterminate flowerheads which form in clusters, like those of lilac (syringa) and skimmia.

Paniculate Like a panicle; arranged and growing in panicles.

Pannose Covered in tiny hairs, feeling like felt or smooth fur.

Papilionaceous Of flowers having the appearance of a butterfly, typified by the leguminous, five-petalled flowers of sweet pea.

Papilla(e) Small, soft protrusion(s).

Papillate Having papillae.

Pappus The fine, tufty whorl of hairs which aids seed dispersal by wind, such as is found in dandelions and other members of the *Compositae* family.

Papula A large pimple or papilla. Also known as papule.

Papyraceous Papery.

Parasite A plant or animal which derives its food and water from another living organism with no benefit to the host, although parasitism does not necessarily mean death for that host.

Biological control makes use of the parasitic nature of some of these organisms, such as nematodes in the control of slugs, for example.

Parenchyma Soft, spongy tissue of plants, often simply called pith and differentiated from tissues which conduct water and nutrients.

Parent/parental generation The plants from which F_1 hybrids are created; this term can also be applied to any plant from which an offspring is derived, whether it be by cutting an offshoot from it or the result of layering.

Paring box A box used to cut turves of grass to a uniform thickness.

Paripinnate A leaf which is pinnate (having leaflets in pairs) but without a leaflet at the tip.

Parrot A type of tulip which is exotic in its colours with scissored-edged petals.

Parrot beak Secateurs with curved blades which overlap.

Parterre A formal garden design of French origins, consisting of level, geometrically laid out beds, often in squares and edged with dwarf box hedging. Low-growing bedding plants typically feature inside the boxes, while grass pathways link the beds. It is a design which can be enjoyed when viewed from a higher level as well as looking beautiful on ground level.

Parthenocarpic Of a plant with the ability to set fruit without having been fertilized, as in the greenhouse cucumber.

Parthenogenesis The development of seeds without fertilization.

Patelliform Saucer-shaped and thickened.

Pathogen Fungi and bacteria or other living organisms which cause plant diseases.

Pathology The study of diseases.

Pea gravel Pea-size stones which are used for gravel paths.

Peat The result of organic matter decomposing in boggy or fenland areas. The conditions in which peat is formed are anaerobic (without air), meaning there is little bacteria present to hasten decomposition. Peat from bogs is lighter in colour and created in acid waters. Fens, on the other hand, neutralize the acidity present and destroy the structure of the plant, making it very black in appearance.

Peat is harvested and sold commercially as a good planting medium, especially for plants that require lime-free soil. Peat has highly absorbent properties, but contains little in the way of nutrients. It is also a good insulator and so can be used to cover the crowns of plants in winter, protecting tender types from frost.

The use of peat in horticulture is a highly controversial subject as it is a resource which renews itself only very slowly. Many gardeners now choose to use alternatives, such as coir or bark, which have similar properties of absorbency and porosity.

Peat bed Usually raised, a bed for lime-hating plants, such as camellias and rhododendrons, made up of loose peat or peat blocks.

Peat block Blocks of peat hewn from peat bogs, used as retaining edges for peat beds.

Peat pot A container made from compressed peat which allows plant roots to penetrate the pot sides, allowing the plant and pot to be planted straight into the ground.

Peck A now obsolete unit of measurement that is actually equivalent to 2 gallons of dry weight or a quarter of a bushel.

Pectinate Meaning toothed like a comb, minutely divided.

Pedate A description of a leaf which is shaped like a bird's foot, palmate with deeply cut lobes.

Pedicel A single flower stalk in a cluster of flowers (inflorescence).

Pedicelled (Pedicellate) Having a pedicel.

Pedogenesis The formation of soil.

Pedology The study of soils.

Peduncle A flower stalk either of a single flower or an inflorescence.

Peeler Any plant which strips the soil of its natural goodness.

Pegging down The practice of bending down long shoots so that their growing tips are at ground level.

Often plants are pegged down for the purposes of layering, whereby shoots form roots in the soil into which they have been pegged.

Pelleted seed Seed which has been deliberately coated with a soluble covering for the purposes of easier handling and even sowing, often because the seed is very small. The covering is inert so does not alter the germination in any way, although sometimes fungicide is incorporated to fend off damping off disease, a common problem of young seedlings.

Pellicle A translucent membrane or skin, usually of a non-cellular nature.

Pelosol A type of soil, also known as a cracking clay. It is this type of soil structure which can cause subsidence, due to its tendency to shrink and expand greatly.

Peltate A leaf which is shaped like a shield with the stem meeting the leaf at the centre of its underside, rather than the top.

Pendent Used with reference to flowers, leaves, branches etc. which hang down instead of being held erect.

Pendulous Hanging down and able to swing loosely.

Penicillate Tufted, brush-shaped.

Penninerved Also penniveined and penniribbed; a feather-like arrangement of veins emanating from the midrib.

Percolation The downward movement of water through soil, drawn by gravity.

Perennate When plants live year after year; overwintering.

Perennial Generally speaking, the term refers to herbaceous or non-woody plants which die down at the end of the growing season and resume life the following spring. Strictly speaking, any plant which lives for more than two years.

Perfect A bisexual flower having all the necessary parts for reproduction.

Perfoliate Paired leaves which grow around a stem and are joined at the base so that the stem appears to grow through the centre of a single leaf, for example, the leaves of tolmeia and juvenile eucalyptus.

Pergola A three-sided, open structure, usually wooden, which covers a path and provides support for climbing plants, such as roses, honeysuckle and wisteria.

Perlite Volcanic rock, expanded by heat, used for adding to compost in granular form because of its properties of absorbency and aeration.

Perpetual Of a plant which blooms continuously over a long season.

Persistent A term that is used in reference to flowers, leaves, berries, etc which remain on a plant for a long time, for example, the berries of skimmia and pyracantha.

Pest A living organism, which jeopardizes the health of plants, for example, insects, viruses and weeds; any organism which causes economic loss or is a nuisance.

   The term is very specific to situations: a pest of one plant might be beneficial to another. For example, most growers would consider honey bees a beneficial insect because of their pollinating activities, however, a cucumber grower, who wants his/her cucumber flowers to remain unfertilized would consider the bee a pest.

Pestology The study of pests.

Petal A leaf corolla; this modified leaf is often bright in colour and a number of them circle the vital reproductive organs of a flower, acting as attractants and landing stages for the pollinating insects.

Petaloid Resembling a petal in shape, colour and texture.

Petiole A leaf stalk.

Petiolulate Possessing a petiolule.

Petiolule The stalk of a leaflet.

pH (value) A unit of measurement of soil acidity and alkalinity, covering 1-6 (acid), 7 (neutral) and 8-14 (alkaline). The more hydrogen ions in the soil, the greater the acidity. Soil test kits are commercially available so that individuals can check the pH of their soil.

Phloem Tissue which transports food in soluble form to all parts of the plant.

Phosphorus A soil element necessary for the development of plant roots, having the chemical symbol P, found in balanced fertilizers (NPK). Plants which lack the element have reduced growth and the leaves become dark green/blue-green and a red pigment may also appear.

Phosphate of potash A fertilizer containing highly concentrated phosphoric acid and potash, used as a liquid manure.

Photoperiodism Plants' ability to sense length of day and night, and the means by which they synchronize their growth cycles with the seasons.

Photosynthesis The process of food manufacture whereby chlorophyll in plant leaves traps the sun's energy, combines it with carbon dioxide in the air and hydrogen in water and creates carbohydrates.

Phyllocladous Refers to stems and branches which function as leaves.

Physiology The functions of all parts of living organisms which are essential for life and growth.

Phyto A prefix which pertains to plant.

Phytophthora A common disease of many ornamental and fruit trees, heathers, rhododendrons and azaleas, and conifers, causing extensive damage to tree roots and ultimately killing the plant. The symptoms are yellowing of foliage and areas of dead bark.

Phytotoxin Any substance which is toxic to plants.

Picotee A flower whose petals have a dark edging around them.

Pig manure A soil fertilizer of less value than other animal fertilizers but nonetheless useful, having rotted down for at least a year. It has a wetter consistency than other animal dung and so is useful for dry, light soils to enhance their water retentiveness.

Pillar A tree trained to have a limited spread of branches, often an apple tree.
   Also, a rose trained up a pole.

Pilose Sparsely covered with fine hair-like growths or down.

Pilosulous Slightly pilose.

Pinching out The practice of removing the growing tip of a plant by pinching the shoot between thumbnail and finger, to encourage sideshoots to grow and thus promote a bushier, more attractive plant. Otherwise known as 'stopping'.

Pinetum This is the term for an arboretum that consists of only conifers for botanical or ornamental purposes.

Pink bud The stage when a plant is in bud – not yet open but showing the colour of the flowers to come.

Pinna A leaflet of a pinnate leaf.

Pinnate Of a leaf – many leaflets that are arranged opposite in pairs, rather like a feather, on both sides of a main stem. The whole structure is the leaf, the small leaves are leaflets.

Pinnatisect Narrower than the leaf division of leaves described as pinnatifid, these leaf divisions are deeply cut near the midrib.

Pippin A term that can be used to describe any variety of apple tree that can be raised from seed.

Piriform Shaped like a pear.

Pit A small, sunken blemish in the skin of a fruit; or, its stone.

Pitch Resinous substance yielded by some fir and pine trees.

Pitcher-shaped Bell-shaped but slightly narrower at the open end.

Pithy A way of referring to a stem that is unripe.

Placenta The ovary wall made up of fused carpels which carry the ovules.

Placentation The position of the ovules inside the placenta. It varies from plant to plant – some have central, some have basal and so on.

Plant To put into the ground for the purpose of growth.

Plants which are grown in containers (which is usually the case when bought from garden centres) can be planted at any time of the year, provided the ground is not frozen or waterlogged and the plant is looked after properly. Bare rootballed plants are normally planted in either spring or autumn – nature's planting time,

when the soil is still warm and there is sufficient moisture.

Generally speaking, whether planting, trees, shrubs or herbaceous perennials or bedding, certain rules should be followed.

The ground should be prepared by adding compost and breaking up the surrounding soil, so that roots can seek out food and water and anchor the plant in the ground.

The plant's roots should be kept moist prior to planting – if containerized place the pot in a bucket of water to ensure the surrounding soil is completely moist.

Always ensure that the planting hole is big enough – do not try to cram the rootball into a space only just big enough, make it $1\frac{1}{2}$ to 2 times as big as the rootball.

Firm in the plant, either with a heel or fists, so that it can't easily be pulled out. If it is loose, there isn't enough compost covering the plant's roots and when it rains the rootball will be left uncovered. This could be detrimental, as the roots can quickly dry out if left exposed to desiccating winds. Also, the wind will easily rock the plant, so that roots will be damaged, especially the small fibrous root hairs which are responsible for most of the food and water uptake.

Always water the plant in immediately afterwards and keep watering on a regular basis thereafter, particularly in dry weather. In the case of trees and shrubs, this can mean for up to two years – until the plant is established.

Plantlet Some plants produce these mini plants on their leaves as a means of reproducing themselves.

Planter An ornamental container for plants, most often for outdoors.

Plant lice Describes any sap-sucking pest, such as aphid.

Plant up A bed or border filled with plants is described as 'planted up'. A pot or container might also be planted up.

Plant out To put a plant into the ground outside; usually said of plants which have been raised under glass.

Plashing/Pleaching The practice of interweaving hedge branches to make a dense screen.

Plastic/Plasticity Of soils, and especially clays, which are extremely mouldable and have cohesion. These types of soil tend to be susceptible to losing their structure and shouldn't be worked after heavy rain.

Plant out To put a plant into the ground outside; usually said of plants which have been raised under glass.

Platy A description of clayey soils with plate-like particles, which make it flaky or leafy.

Plicate Folded like a closed fan.

Plumose Feathery.

Plunge To place a pot plant up to its rim into a bed or frame of soil or other material, such as sand or peat, to protect its roots from extremes of heat or cold.

Bulbs required for early indoor use, such as hyacinths, can also be plunged in a shady bed to bring on an early display, by completely covering bulbs to a depth of 7.5-12.5cm (3-5in).

Tender plants that are grown in pots can be plunged in outside borders still in their pots, to add to a summer display, and then brought back under glass for winter protection.

Plunge bench Bench for plunging pots in.

Pneumatophore Some plants which exist near or in water develop breathing roots which protrude like knobbly knees above the surface of the water, for example the swamp cypress, *Taxodium distichum*.

There is, however, some doubt as to the necessity of these roots as research shows their removal does not seem to damage the plant in any way.

Pod A term that is generally applied to any dry, splitting fruit.

Podzolic A type of soil which has an acid, organic layer on its surface, commonly represented by heathland, where the leaf litter is derived from heathers and pines. It doesn't become mixed into the soil, because of the lack of earthworms in the acid soil.

Poisonous plants Plants which contain chemicals that can cause adverse reactions and in rare cases, fatalities in humans and animals when ingested. Many plants which are safe to eat have parts which are dangerously poisonous, for example, the leaves of rhubarb.

Care should be taken when planting up a garden if children and pets are going to frequent it. Common poisonous plants include: laburnum, monkshood, yew and castor oil plant.

Other plants contain sap which irritates the skin, for example, ruta and euphorbia, and gloves should always be worn whenever they are being handled.

Polesaw A long-handled pruning saw for lopping high-up branches.

Pollard (Poll) To cut back a tree to the top of its trunk in order to renew its growth. A practice that is used on street trees when branches are becoming hazardous or blocking daylight from house interiors. It is condemned by some as a brutal and ugly practice.

It is also used commercially to encourage young, straight shoots.

Pollen Spores which are attached to the anthers inside a flower. They fertilize the ovule.

Pollination Refers to the transference of pollen from the male anthers to the female stigma. This process is carried out by insects, such as bees, and also by the wind.

Pollinator Any agent which brings about pollination.

Pollution Soot and particles from car exhausts and industry land on plant leaves and block stomata (pores). This impedes important gaseous exchange and prevents light reaching the chlorophyll, which means that leaves are less able to create food.

Sulphur dioxide in the air combines with water which leads to acid rain and causes extensive and long-lasting damage to plants.

Some plants are better able to cope with pollution than others, and these make useful plants for city streets. For example, periwinkle (*Vinca major* and *minor*), hydrangeas, camellias and *Prunus laurocerasus*.

Polyadelphous Having many stamens which are united into one bundle.

Polycarpic Fruiting many times; or fruiting year after year.

Polygamodioecious Bearing both male, female and bisexual flowers.

Polygamous Plant species in which male, female and hermaphrodite flowers appear on the same plant.

Polypetalous Having a corolla made up of separate petals.

Polyploid Possessing more than the standard two sets of chromosomes.

Polysepalous Having a calyx with sepals arranged separately.

Polystyrene This is used in granular form in potting compost for its excellent aeration qualities.

Polytrichous Hairy.

Polytunnel A polythene-covered frame for growing plants. Popular commercially, they are also available to amateurs as less expensive alternatives to greenhouses.

Pome A fruit in which the seeds are encased in a tough covering (the wall of the carpel) and then also by a fleshy outer covering.

Pomology The study of fruit growing.

Pomiferous Bearing fruit, especially apples or other pomes.

Pom-pom Describes a type of round flower, used as a classification for dahlias and chrysanthemums.

Pond liners Either a rigid plastic mould for the purpose of holding water or impervious plastic sheeting trimmed to the size of the pond.

Pore A hole in a leaf which takes in carbon dioxide and emits oxygen. Leaves have many of these apertures, which open and close by the action of stoma.

Porous Having many pores and therefore permeable to liquids.

Porrect Stretching outwards.

Potash nitrate A soluble fertilizer containing nitrogen and potash, suitable for application in spring and early summer.

Potassium/Potash A soil element that is essential for the successful development of flowers and fruit. Its chemical symbol is K, one of the three elements of a balanced fertilizer, NPK.

Potato leaf roll The symptoms of this common virus are rolled leaves and stunting of tuber growth.
    Planting less susceptible varieties and controlling aphids in the area can prevent attacks. Dazomet, a soil-sterilant, may be worth using where large crops are grown.

Potato planter A pair of tongs for planting potatoes. The action of opening them opens up the soil, then the potato tuber is inserted, and the action of closing the tongs allows the soil to fall back into its original place.

Pot bound This occurs when the roots of a container-grown plant have run out of space in their pot and are therefore constrained by it. Roots can sometimes be seen coming out of the bottom of the pot and once the rootball is knocked out, the roots are seen to be matted and may have started to grow round in the shape of the bottom of the pot. Usually, plants should be potted on to the next size pot, freeing the roots slightly at the same time. Some plants, however, prefer being slightly pot bound as this emulates their natural conditions, such as the jungle floor, where they would constantly have to compete with the roots of other plants.

Pot on Moving a pot plant to the pot next up in size.

Never use a pot which is much larger than the one it has been used to as root problems may occur.

Pot plant Containerized plants, grown in pots and not intended for planting in the open ground – usually house plants.

Pot pourri A mixture of dried aromatic leaves and flowers used as air fresheners.

Potting Placing seedlings and rooted cuttings into their first pots after they have been pricked out.

Potting bench A special three-sided bench for working on while potting plants.

Potworm A root-damaging worm that is found in the unsterilized soil of container grown plants.

Poultry manure Chicken waste used as an organic fertilizer. It is thought that chickens which have been farmed under intensive conditions produce more concentrated manure.

Powdery mildew A fungus which appears as a powdery coating on the upper surfaces of leaves, stems and buds, usually in warm dry periods. It isn't generally a killer but causes distorted and discoloured growth. It can be treated at fortnightly intervals with a systemic fungicide, such as triforine or benomyl.

Pre-emergent weedkillers Weedkillers that can be used after seed has been sown, but prior to germination.

Pre-sprouting As in chitting, seeds are placed on a piece of blotting paper to germinate prior to sowing.

Early to flower or set fruit; flowers which appear before the leaves, for example, those of *Magnolia* x *soulangeana*.

Predator Insects that prey upon other insects are becoming increasingly useful in horticulture. Biological control exploits these natural relationships between insects to get rid of unwanted pests. For example, a tiny wasp, *Encarsia formosa*, is a natural predator of whitefly, a common pest of house and greenhouse plants.

Prefabricated pond A fibreglass or plastic pond, usually fitted with ledges to hold marginal plants in baskets.

Digging out a site for a prefabricated pond requires a certain amount of care as the ponds are usually quite intricate shapes. They should be shaped as closely as possible, and stones should be removed. A base of sand should be put down to mould into the shape of the pond.

Premorse/praemorse Having the end abruptly terminated, as in a leaf.

Prepared Bulbs which flower indoors at Christmas are prepared or forced to bloom earlier than they would in nature. Bulbs can only be prepared in this way once, and if they are put outside for the following year, they may not flower in their first year.

Pricking out The spacing of seedlings which have their first true leaves, or even just their first two dicotyledon leaves, into pots or further seedtrays. This is to prevent overcrowding of small seedlings, which have to compete for light, and to avoid fungal problems.

Pricking out is effected by taking hold of a leaf, not the stem as this can easily damage the vital food and water-carrying vessels, and pushing a dibber or pencil next to the seedling into the soil. Then, the seedling, together with the soil, is lifted up with the dibber, and placed into a new hole made by the dibber or pencil.

Prickle A sharp point which grows from the epidermis of a plant.

Primary Describes first stages of growth.

Primocane The flowering stem or branch of a biennial in its first year of growth.

Priority In the taxonomical naming of plants a rule exists whereby the first published name of a plant is held to be the correct one.

Prism-like Of clay soils which have a prismatic, elongated particle structure. This type of soil is commonly found as sub-soil, particularly on semi-arid land.

Procumbent A term used to describe the habit of a plant which closely hugs the ground, like prostrate.

Projecting Exserting; used mainly of flowerparts which stick out from inside the corolla.

Prokaryote A primitive type of cell, such as that of blue–green algae, where the DNA inside the nucleus is not separated from the rest of the material located in the inside.

Proliferation When a plant produces new shoots, offsets or runners that may in themselves become new plants.

Prominent Conspicuous, raised up from the surface – often used to describe certain plant characteristics, such as the veins on leaves.

Prong cultivator A three-pronged, long-handled tool or hoe used for cultivating the soil.

Propapacks Compartmentalized trays for growing seedlings.

Prop root A root which emanates from a point on the stem above soil level to provide support for the plant, for example the baobab tree.

Propagate To raise plants, from seed, bulbs, cuttings, division, layering etc.

Propagator One who propagates plants. More specifically, a heated or unheated covered box in which plants can be raised. At the bottom end of the range are basic seedtrays with a transparent lid and manual vents. Conversely, electric thermostatically controlled propagators are available for raising plants which require exactly controlled heat and a moist atmosphere in which to germinate.

Propagule Any part of a plant which is used in the process of self-propagation.

Prostrate Like procumbent, lying flat on the ground; describes a plant's low-growing habit.

Protandrous Of a flower whose anthers release pollen before the stigma is actually mature enough to receive it, presumably to avoid self-pollination. Where both are ready at the same time for the purposes of self-pollination, it is known as incomplete protandry.

Protection Tender plants require protection from frost in winter. This might involve placing bracken or straw over the crown of a plant which has died down. Conversely if there is a risk of frozen or waterlogged soil, it is best given the protection of a cold frame or heated greenhouse, depending on how low a temperature the plant in question can cope with.

Protogynous Said of a flower when its stigma is ready to be pollinated before the anthers of the same flower are ready to release the pollen, presumably to avoid self-pollination.

Protruding Sticking out; for example, when stamens are longer than the petals and project beyond the flower.

Proximal The nearest inner part.

Proximate Next to, close by.

Pruinose Covered with a white or waxy bloom, giving a frosted appearance.

Pruning The removal of stems from (usually) woody plants. This may be necessary for a number of reasons: because a plant has become overgrown and needs tidying; to remove dead and diseased or straggly stems because if left the disease might spread; stems that cross and chafe each other must be cut out as this creates an open wound inviting disease, and dense growth prevents light from reaching photosynthesizing leaves.

Pruning is also an aesthetic pursuit, making plants more shapely and taken to extremes is known as 'topiary'.

Pruning is a controversial practice – some gardeners believe that it is not necessary, for if a tree or shrub is planted in the right place it should not become restricted for space and therefore should not need cutting back. After all pruning does not occur in nature, apart from when adverse weather tears branches from plants.

Most pruning takes place in the spring and autumn.

Pruning tools include secateurs and pruning knives for anything under 12mm ($\frac{1}{2}$ in); more than that and a pruning saw is required; trees may need chainsaws but these should really be used only by trained professionals wearing the correct protective clothing.

Pseudanthium An apparently simple flower which, in fact, is made up of more than one axis with further flowers.

Pseudobulb Literally a 'false bulb', this is the bulb-like area of the stem of some plants, for example epiphytic orchids and some terrestrials. The area is used to store food.

Pseudocopulation The attempts of a male insect to mate with the female part of a plant which looks like the female insect of that species. In this way the plant becomes pollinated.

Pseudoscorpion A type of soil organism.

Pseudostem A 'stem' which looks like a branch or trunk but is actually made of overlapping basal leaves, such as in the trunk of the banana tree (*Musa acuminata*).

Pseudoterminal When used in reference to a bud, this is one which takes the place of a damaged or removed bud. In reference to flowers, it is one positioned at the top of a stem but on a lateral.

Psyllids Small insects of the *Hemiptera* group, the adults and larvae of which feed on the sap of leaves, stems and other parts of many plants, causing damage and leaving excreted honeydew and the inevitable sooty mould behind.

Puberulent Slightly downy. Also known as puberulous.

Pubescent Covered with hair or down.

Puddling The practice of wetting clay and compressing it to line a pond. The compression ruins the soil's structure, pressing all the air out of the clay, making it fairly watertight.

Puffy A descriptive term used in relation to chalky soils which contain a great deal of organic matter.

Pulp The pithy centre of some fruit.

Pulse The edible seed of any leguminous plant (those of the *Leguminosae* family), such as chick peas, lentils and peas.

Pulverulent The powdery appearance of some plants' leaves and stems.

Pulvinate Cushion-shaped or swollen.

Pulvinus A cushion of tissue at the base of the petiole which can cause movement by changes in its turgidity; it is sometimes responsive to changes in outside conditions, such as temperature and light.

Punctate Pitted with small spots.

Pungent Meaning terminated by a sharp, hard point.

Pustule An eruption, like a blister or spot.

Pustuliform Like a pustule or blister.

Pyramid/Pyramidal A type of fruit tree that is good for small gardens – the name refers to its habit.

A reference to the triangular shape which some trees naturally attain, for example, *Picea abies*, the Christmas tree.

Pyrene The nutlet of a drupe.

Pyrethrum An organic insecticide, made from the flowers of pyrethrum.

Pyriform See Piriform.

Q

Quadrat A square frame used to define a specific area and used to determine the density and diversity of plants and animals in that area.

Quadrageneric Plant with four different genera in its ancestry.

Quadrangular Term used to describe parts of a plant that are four angled – such as the passion flower stem (*Passiflora*).

Quagmire An area of land that is boggy or marshy.

Quassia Natural bird, insect and animal repellant derived from the wood of the tropical tree *Picrasma excelsa*. Wood chips are boiled in water to produce an obnoxious and extremely bitter brew which is then diluted and applied as a heavy spray or drench. A deterrent rather than a cure.

Quatrefoil A flower with four petals or a leaf composed of four leaflets.

Queach A dense thicket or hedge.

Quercetum A collection or plantation of trees of the oak family (*Quercus*).

Quicklime A compound made by burning chalk, limestone or shells in a kiln to produce calcium oxide. Somewhat caustic to plants and unpleasant to handle but can be mixed with water to produce hydrated lime which can be applied to vacant soil to raise pH levels.

Also known as lump lime.

Quilled A term used to describe leaves or petals which are tubular for much of their length. Cactus dahlias are a good example.

Quinsy-berry The ancient name for the blackcurrant, possibly derived from a medicinal use as a treatment for throat infections.

R

Raceme Generally pointed flowerhead where individual flowers are carried on short lateral stems from a single unbranched main stem. Lupin, hyacinth and foxglove are good examples and flowers usually open at the base first, gradually progressing to the tip.

Radical A term used to describe part of a plant that is growing from the root or at the base of a stem.

Radicle The first root produced by a germinating seed, or arising directly from the root of a plant.

Raffia A fibre obtained from the African palm known as *Raphia ruffa*, which is extremely soft and was once widely used as a plant tie. Now largely superseded by twine or string, raffia is still available and is a more 'natural' alternative. Its soft, pliable texture means that it can be used on the youngest shoots without causing damage.

Raft Term used to describe a piece of bark or branch, onto which epiphytic plants, such as tillandsias, and orchids are wired for display purposes.

Raised bed Artificially made flower bed for cultivation of ornamental or productive crops. Especially useful if the natural soil level is prone to waterlogging or is unsuitable for particular plants such as alpines. Also ideal for aged and disabled gardeners as it allows easier access.

Rake This must be one of the most essential garden tools and it is available in a variety of forms.

The most popular is a rigid metal form with teeth about 2.5cm (1in) long and which is at right angles to the head. Used to break down the soil prior to sowing, it will also level and remove stones at the same time. A good eye and long sweeping movements produce the best results on soil that is drying out but not bone dry. Raking should not be carried out in wet conditions in order to avoid problems with compaction.

Larger wooden, cane or plastic rakes with flexible teeth arranged as a fan are used for collecting up grass clippings, fallen leaves and other light debris. Wire forms are also used to remove moss from lawns without causing too much damage to the grass.

Rambler A type of rose that produces long, vigorous shoots that can be allowed to climb trellis, pergolas or other plants such as large shrubs and trees.

Ramentaceous A term used to describe leaves and stems that are covered in small, brown scales.

Ramification Used to describe the arrangement and spread of a tree's branches.

Ramiflorus A plant that produces flowers directly on larger branches and bare twigs, but not the main trunk.

Ramose Divided into many branches.

Raspberry beetle Small greyish or golden brown beetle that attacks the flowers of raspberries and lays its eggs. These hatch later and the maggots immediately feed on the developing raspberry fruits. Spraying with a suitable insecticide at flowering time and again a couple of weeks later will solve the problem.

Ratoon Used to describe the cutting down of a plant to ground level in order to encourage new shoots to begin forming.

A sucker or new shoot growing from the base of a plant.

Ray-floret The flowers of some members of the daisy family (*Compositae*) have flowers that are surrounded by showier florets, each with a strap–shaped corolla.

Recessive A characteristic not exhibited by a plant but carried by its genetic material. In subsequent generations, the characteristic may become apparent if both parents carry the 'recessive gene'.

Recumbent Term used to describe a plant's habit of lying along the ground.

Recurved, Reflexed Referring to leaves or petals that are curved downwards.

Reflexed also refers to a more acute curvature.

Red spider mite A tiny mite (acarina), barely visible to the human eye, that colonizes all types of plants, but is most noticeable on house plants that are growing in hot, dry conditions. With a magnifying glass they will be seen to be reddish black with round bodies and eight legs. The mites suck the sap of the leaves, usually from the undersides and produce a fine webbing over the leaves and petioles. Leaves take on a mottled appearance and fall prematurely.

Increasing ventilation and humidity (by misting) will help prevent attack. A suitable insecticide should be applied at the first sign of infestation and repeated as necessary.

Red thread A fungal lawn disease identified by the red thread-like growths that develop on the grass accompanied by irregular discoloured patches. A sign of nitrogen deficiency; an application of fertilizer will usually be sufficient.

Regulatory pruning The removal of weak, diseased or overcrowded growth as necessary.

Remontant Some plants have a second flush of flower and are termed 'remontant'. The second display is usually slightly inferior to the first. Roses are an extremely good example.

Reniform Refers to leaves that are kidney shaped. Zonal pelargoniums are a good example of this.

Repand A botanical term used to describe petal and leaf edges that are slightly wavy in outline.

Repand–denticulate Slightly wavy as with repand but with the addition of finely toothed margins.

Repot Moving a plant from one pot to another, usually slightly larger to provide fresh compost and room for additional root growth.

Resinous A plant that contains or exudes resin, for example, conifers.

Resistant Able to withstand certain outside influences. This may be an ability to withstand certain diseases, or factors like the cold. Plant breeders have worked hard to improve hardiness of plants and their ability to withstand a wide range of diseases to make the gardener's life easier and limit the use of chemicals. However, the term 'resistant' means just that – the plants are not immune.

Respiration The natural process whereby plants absorb carbon dioxide from the atmosphere and expire oxygen during the day, and absorb oxygen and expire carbon dioxide during the night. Part of the process of 'photosynthesis'.

Resting period Nearly all plants have a dormant period where there is no active growth. Bulbs are a good example; when they die down after flowering they will remain 'resting' for several months. This resting period is essential for good subsequent growth giving the bulbs time to ripen and prepare themselves for the cold winter and a surge of growth in spring. Deciduous trees exhibit a similar characteristic over the winter months.

However, some plants (such as house plants which are really more tender species growing in a very artificial environment) do not have a marked resting period although there is usually a period of slower growth – normally when temperatures and light levels are lower during the winter.

Retarding A way of fooling plants into flowering at a later date – usually through keeping them at lower temperatures for longer than natural. 'Prepared' bulbs are a good example: they can be planted in the autumn and will flower in time for Christmas. Hyacinths and narcissus that would normally be starting into growth in the autumn are kept dry and cold until the following summer. They are then brought out of storage and, once planted and given normal temperatures and moisture, will make extremely rapid growth and flower within a few weeks.

Commercially, many economic crops are retarded to provide an all-year-round crop. This is now done using special hormone sprays. Similarly, seed potatoes are retarded with a special hormone to stop them sprouting too early.

Reticulate Derived from the Latin word meaning netted. Used to describe flowers or leaves with net-like or branched markings or veining.

Retuse A term that is used to describe the shape of leaves that have a rounded or notched end.

Reversion Term used to describe a change in a plant's appearance. This may be because the rootstock becomes more vigorous – outgrowing the grafted variety – or because the form is unstable, such as when a variegated plant produces a plain green shoot. Being green and being able to photosynthesize more easily, these green shoots can rapidly outgrow the variegated part of the plant.

With blackcurrants, the term 'reversion' is rather misleading. It originates from when a disorder was identified and it was wrongly thought that the currants were reverting to their original type. In fact it

refers to a virus which reduces cropping and can be identified by a reduction in the number of veins in the leaves. If there are fewer than five pairs of veins on the leaves and if leaves at the end of the branches are crowded together, the bush is probably suffering from reversion.

Revolute A term used to describe the rolling under – most usually of the edges of a leaf.

Rhizome A fleshy underground stem that acts as a storage organ so the plant may rest during the winter months, for example bearded iris. Each year the rhizome produces buds and shoots from the end so the older part dies and shrivels.

The term is also sometimes used to refer to overground shoots that then root some distance from the parent plant. Couch grass is the most obvious example.

Rhizome rot A disease which affects early summer-flowering irises. Those that have been most badly affected should be lifted and burned. If damage is minor, the affected part can be cut away using a sharp knife.

Rhomboidal A term used to describe leaves that are roughly diamond shaped.

Rhubarb pot A large terracotta pot inverted over rhubarb plants to encourage early, succulent, blanched growth.

Rib A surface protrusion of the leaf caused by the veins. Some stems may also be ribbed, for example, in some cacti.

Riddle Another term for a type of sieve which grades soil that is to be used for compost. Generally the mesh size is larger than that found in a sieve.

Ridging Useful on heavy soil, this is a digging method where the soil is thrown up into a ridge exposing a greater surface area to the elements. The weather (and especially frost) can then break it down. Ridges are then raked level prior to planting in the spring.

Rind The layer of bark, outside the 'cambium' layer.

Ring culture The ring in this instance refers to a bottomless pot which is filled with compost. This is placed on a bed of ash, peat, sand, gravel or expanded clay granules that are supplied with water and nutrients throughout the growing season. This method of cultivation requires less compost and gives the grower greater control over nutrient levels. Although largely a commercial technique, some amateur gardeners have found results on a domestic scale to be encouraging.

Ringing Used to reduce the vigour of plants – especially fruit trees. In mid to late spring, a thin strip of bark is removed from the main trunk about 60cm (2ft) above the ground. In this way the flow of nutrients from the tree to its roots is partially interrupted and growth reduced. This encourages the tree to produce more flower buds, leading to heavier cropping. Partial ringing is where two half rings are removed – one slightly above the other, resulting in a less dramatic result. Simpler still is knife ringing where a blade is drawn round, cutting through the bark. This can be used on individual branches and stems.

Ripening When referring to the shoot of woody plants, the term 'ripening' refers to the thickening of the plant tissues as the season progresses.

With fruit, the term refers to the maturing of the fruit, in preparation for seed dispersal.

Rock garden An area of the garden which has been set aside and used to create an artificial environment, mimicking the conditions that are preferred by species of alpine plants.

Many different types of rock are used but the site should always be away from any shade. Soil should be very free drain-ing but moisture-retentive: incorporating generous amounts of horticultural grit will suffice. To achieve good drainage on wet soil and clay it may be necessary to install an artificial drainage system to pre-vent waterlogging, or to raise the rock garden above the natural soil level with the help of retaining walls.

The term 'rockery' is often used, although this is usually applied to rock gardens where very little or no attempt has been made to recreate a natural landscape by the careful positioning of rocks.

Rock plant An alpine plant that is particularly suitable for growing in the rock garden. The term is also applied to small perennials, bulbs, shrubs and conifers.

Rod An old measurement of length equal to 16 $\frac{1}{2}$ ft (approx 5m) and equal to a pole and perch. Many allotment sites were originally laid out in rods and the rents worked out accordingly.

Rod is also a term used to refer to the main stem of a grape vine.

Rogue Any plant that does not look as it is supposed to. This is usually the result of accidental mixing of seeds, bulbs, etc. prior to planting. Good suppliers of seeds and bulbs will make every endeavour to ensure that rogues do not occur.

Roller A large iron or water-filled plastic drum used to level the surface of lawns (and occasionally soil). It should never be used in wet conditions as the soil will quickly become compacted, and nor should it be used when the soil is bone dry. Most cylinder movers include some sort of roller, although in this case, the levelling effect is minimal and they really only help to produce the much sought-after striped effect on the finished lawn.

Spiked rollers are used to aerate the soil in early autumn and the nail-like tines dig into the soil alleviating any compaction. A dressing of sharp sand should be applied afterwards to fill the spike holes with a free-draining material.

Rond point The point in a formal garden where the paths, avenues or vistas in a geometric design meet. Usually a round paved area with some form of focal point or a circular pool.

Root The subterranean part of a plant that provides the plant's support and feeds the plant by absorbing nutrients and water from the surrounding soil. Roots may also serve as storage organs.

Rootball A term used to describe the soil held by the plant's roots. When you are lifting or planting, the rootball should be handled carefully to prevent damage to the fine feeding roots.

Root crop A plant grown for its fleshy, edible roots.

Root cutting Propagation of a plant using a section of root. Good for fleshy rooted perennials such as oriental poppies and hollyhocks. Taken while the plant is dormant, sections of root approximately 5cm

(2 $\frac{1}{2}$ in) long are removed, making a straight cut nearest the plant and a slanting cut at the other end. This way it is possible to keep the cuttings the right way up as shoots will develop from the point that was nearest to the plant. If the cutting is inserted in a free draining compost (straight cut uppermost) and placed in a garden frame over winter, buds and shoots will develop in spring.

Rooting medium Any substance, such as compost, peat, sand, perlite or vermiculite in which cuttings can produce roots.

Rooting powder Powder containing a synthetic plant hormone that encourages root formation on cuttings. Sometimes referred to as 'hormone rooting powder', it may also contain a fungicide. Liquid formulations are also available.

Root pruning A method of reducing the vigour of a plant by depriving it of some of its supply of water and nutrients. Once a common practice with fruit trees, it has been largely replaced by the use of restrictive rootstocks which also limit the vigour of the plants grafted onto them.

Autumn is considered the best time to root prune. A trench should be taken out about 30cm (1ft) deep in a circle level with the ends of the branches of the plant. Soil should be removed with a fork to expose the roots and the thickest can be cut with a sharp pair of secateurs. Any

thinner or fibrous roots should be left intact. For a less dramatic check to growth half the circumference can be done one year, and the other half subsequently.

Root rot A term used to describe a number of diseases, all of which attack the plant's roots causing the top growth to wither and die. The most notorious is honey fungus – so named because of the honey-coloured mushrooms that appear above the soil. The fungus below ground resembles black bootlaces and attacks the roots of woody plants and eventually kills them.

Generally root rots are the result of fungal infection because of physical damage and/or poor drainage.

Root run The extent to which the roots of a plant spread. This is largely influenced by the soil condition and fertility, with plants in poor, free-draining soil travelling much further than those in nutrient-rich, moisture-retentive soils. In general, the roots of a healthy plant extend at least as far as the top growth is wide.

Root scorch Damage to the roots of a plant through the application of a high concentration of fertilizer. Growth is usually checked although in severe cases the plant may die.

Root stock The roots onto which a grafted variety of plant is placed. Many fruit trees are grafted onto rootstocks which are naturally less vigorous and will therefore stunt the growth of the tree. This is particularly useful for restricted forms, such as cordons, fans and espaliers, and for smaller gardens generally. Many trees and shrubs are also grafted onto specific rootstocks – sometimes to reduce vigour, but more commonly because they are naturally poor rooting themselves.

Rosary Victorian term used to describe a rose garden or a collection of roses in a mixed planting.

Rose A perforated watering can attachment used to produce a finer spray of water droplets necessary when watering young plants and seedlings.

Rose aphid An aphid that is specific to roses and which sucks the sap of young shoots, leaves and flowers, causing distortion. Can be effectively controlled using a suitable insecticide.

Rosette A term used to describe the arrangement of petals or leaves when they form a tight circle or spiral or resemble the arrangement found in a rose.

Rot To decompose or decay. Stressed or damaged plant tissue will rot leading to eventual death and decay.

Rotary cultivator An easier method of cultivating the soil than digging is to use a powered cultivator. Rotary cultivators have a series of blades or tines that revolve, turning the soil and bringing weeds and stones to the surface. While the effect is dramatic and large areas can be covered in a fraction of the time taken to dig, rotary cultivators do not solve deep-rooted drainage or panning problems.

Rotary mower A lawnmower that relies on two or four blades which rotate level to the surface of the lawn. They rely on high speed impact to cut the grass rather than a scissor action (as with cylinder mowers).

They may be wheeled or hover on a cushion of air and are recommended for normal lawns rather than those with a high grade sward. They can also be used effectively on sloping lawns.

Rotation Different vegetable crops take different nutrients from the soil. A rotation system ensures that crops are grown on different plots each year. Some crops like freshly manured and fertilized soil, while others are happiest on ground that was manured for an earlier crop. Any build-up of pests and disease will also be eliminated.

Although restricted by available space, it is possible to adopt a basic three-year rotation system on the domestic vegetable plot. By dividing the land into three equal portions and devoting one area to brassicas, one to potatoes and the third mainly to root crops, a system of rotation can be achieved. The brassica plot should receive generous applications of animal manure and compost, and nitrogen–rich feed can be applied during the growing season. The potato area can also receive the manure and compost but needs a more balanced application of fertilizers – preferably one that is higher in phosphate. The third area should receive no compost or manure, just an application of a fertilizer that is lower in nitrogen. In the second year, the potatoes are followed by the brassicas, the root crop area should be used for the potatoes and the root crops moved to where the brassicas were.

Rotenone The active ingredient found in derris, which is itself derived from the roots of certain tropical plants. The higher the concentration of rotenone in the derris, the more effective it will be.

Rotting agent A compound used to speed up the process of decomposition in the compost heap.

Rotund Rounded in appearance; curved like a circle.

Ruderal Term used to describe plants that are found growing on waste land and near rubbish heaps.

Rudimentary Term describing plant parts that are undeveloped or non-functional.

Rufescent Reddish-brown in appearance.

Rugose The botanical term meaning wrinkled, often referring to leaves. Sometimes Latinized as a specific name – such as *Rosa rugosa*.

Runcinate A botanical term used to describe flowers or leaves that have large, downward-facing points or teeth.

Runner Plants produce various specialized shoots and a runner is a specialized stem that grows along the surface of the ground making roots from buds which appear at intervals along it. Examples include violets, bugle (*Ajuga* – excellent ground cover), strawberries (where these runners are often encouraged to root to provide more plants) and creeping buttercup (a pernicious weed).

On cultivated plants runners should generally be removed to maintain the vigour of the original plant. Only for propagation should selected runners be allowed to root.

Russet A rough brown velvety covering of the skin – often found on apples and pears; it may be a natural characteristic or the result of climatic or physical damage.

Rust In horticultural terms this refers to a number of diseases all of which produce rust-coloured spots or pustules on affected plants. Antirrhinums, hollyhocks, roses and carnations are particularly susceptible. Affected leaves should be removed and an appropriate fungicide applied, although control is limited.

Plant breeders have worked hard to include disease resistance in their breeding programmes and rust resistant varieties are now available.

S

Saddle graft A type of graft where an inverted 'V' is cut in both stock and scion. The scion has just one terminal bud and the two portions, which should match as far as possible, are bound together until a union forms.

Sagittate A word meaning arrow-shaped, used to describe the leaves of plants. A pointed triangle with one point forward and two backwards.

Salicetum A group or planting of willows (*Salix*). Also referred to as a 'sally-wood' or 'sally-garden'.

Saline Containing salt. The rain, wind and soil in coastal regions are often laden with salt and may be referred to as 'saline'.

Saltpetre The common name for potassium nitrate more usually referred to as nitrate of potash.

Sampler A single young tree left standing after those around it have been felled.

Sand Used horticulturally to improve drainage of poor soils; the grittier the sand the better. Can also be used as a rooting medium for seeds and cuttings when it is often mixed with perlite or vermiculite although young seedlings and rooted cuttings must be potted on quickly as the sand mix contains no nutrients.

Sap The fluid found in plant cells. It is predominantly water but also contains dissolved sugars and mineral salts.

Sapling Any young tree that hasn't formed any heartwood.

Saprophyte A parasitic plant that lives on decaying matter. Best examples are fungi, and all contain no chlorophyll so are unable to manufacture their own food by photosynthesis. Of great benefit to the gardener, they initiate the breakdown of organic matter in compost heaps.

Sarmentose A term used to describe plants that produce long slender stolons.

Saw Much like the traditional carpenter's tool, the most common garden saw is the pruning saw. These often work in reverse to conventional saws in that the teeth are set so the cutting action is on the pulling stroke rather than when the saw is pushed away. The blades are usually fairly narrow to allow easy access to awkward branches and are often curved for a more effective cutting action.

Keeping the blade clean and the teeth sharp will make life much easier.

Sawfly A term used to describe a variety of fly-like insects, the most common being

the apple sawfly whose larvae are the white maggots that bore into the fruit causing it to fall prematurely. Ribbon-like scars on the fruit develop as the apple swells.

The rose sawfly has a different effect in that it rolls the leaves around itself as a form of protection.

Hand picking these insects off plants and the use of suitable insecticides will prevent or control attacks.

Saxicolous A term used to describe plants that are naturally found growing on or among rocks.

Scab Most common on apples and pears, this refers to the visual effects of a variety of fungal diseases which can attack the young shoots, leaves and fruits. The scabs resemble blisters.

Potato scab fungus is carried in the soil and affects the skin of the tubers making them unsightly and drastically reducing the crop yield. This problem is more prevalent on alkaline soil.

Scabrous A term that means 'harsh to the touch'. This may be because the plant, or part of it, is covered in small scales, teeth or bristles.

Scalding A grape disorder where the grapes shrivel, caused by sun scorch and prevented by shading.

Scalding also refers to a disorder of house and greenhouse plants affected by rapid temperature fluctuations, draughts, hot dry atmospheres and the fumes from paraffin heaters. Leaf edges brown and wither, white or brown spots appear evenly over the leaf surface, young shoots wither and brown and fruits shrivel. Pay attention to cultural conditions and scalding shouldn't be a problem, and plants will recover.

Scale insects A variety of insects that protect themselves during part of their life cycle, limpet-fashion, with a tough outer scale. They suck the sap from stems and leaves.

Fruit trees can be protected with a tar oil winter wash and generally a suitable systemic insecticide will control most infestations. Isolated outbreaks can be removed by hand.

Scandent A term used to describe a plant that scrambles and climbs, but which is not self-clinging.

Scape Flower stems growing directly from the ground that carry no leaves. Best example is *Amaryllis belladonna*.

Scarify To scarify means to rake over the ground to break up its surface. Preparation of a seedbed could be termed 'scarification'.

The second, more common, meaning, is the removal of dead grass, old clippings and moss from the surface of a lawn with a rake to allow easier penetration of water to the soil below.

(Similarly, nicking the seed coat of hard seeds to allow easier germination is also termed scarification.)

Sciarid fly The larvae of small winged insects, sciarid flies live in moist peaty conditions and eat the roots and stems of young plants.

Also referred to as fungus gnats and peat flies, they can be controlled with a suitable insecticide.

Scion/Stock A shoot or bud that is taken from one plant and attached to the roots of another plant.

This process of grafting or budding is used extensively with ornamentals and fruit where the characteristics of one plant are enhanced by the root characteristics of another (ie the scion wood of a vigorous apple is kept in check by the dwarfing characteristics of a particular rootstock). The graft union is usually visible at the base of the plant, or with some standards where the branches are attached to the top of the main trunk.

Great care should be taken to remove any shoots that arise from the rootstock as these are usually more vigorous and can overrun the more desirable grafted variety.

This process is used to propagate plants that will not come true from seed, have naturally poor roots or are difficult to propagate from cuttings.

Scissors There are several types of scissors specifically designed for the gardener. The most important are used for thinning out developing bunches of grapes and are pointed to give easy access. These are called vine scissors. There are also flower gathering scissors, which grip the cut flowers and bonsai scissors designed to cope with intricate work on small leaves, shoots and branches.

Sclerosis A process whereby the walls of cells become hardened and woody.

Sclerotina rot Another name for 'stem rot'.

Scorch Leaves quickly turn brown and dry as a result of bright sunlight, hot weather, cold winds or chemical spray damage. An excess of fertilizer can also have a similar effect.

Scree A mass of rocky debris at the base of a mountain or rock face. Small shards of stone are eroded from the large rocks by the action of frost and rain. These smaller rocks accumulate to form scree beds.

Alpine plants colonize such areas where there is excellent drainage and little humus.

Such an environment can be re-created in the garden and is a good alternative to a rock garden where stone is impractical or too expensive.

A 'moraine' is similar but technically refers to beds of small stones deposited by retreating glaciers.

Screen A hedge, wall, fence or trellis used to hide something from view.

May also be used to define different areas of the garden, provide wind protection to other plants or act as a support for climbing plants.

Scurfy A term used to describe a plant (or part of a plant) that is covered in flour-like scales.

Scythe A bladed hand tool that is swung in a sweeping action level with the ground to cut long grass or clear an area of undergrowth. Now almost completely replaced by powered lawnmowers, trimmers and brushcutters that do a similar job with less effort and require the minimum of user skill.

Sea-kale pot A terracotta pot used for forcing a crop of young blanched stems of sea-kale. Similar in appearance and function to a rhubarb-forcing pot.

Seaweed Used extensively as a manure in the past and regaining popularity with the advent of the organic gardening movement. High in potash, seaweed manures can be applied to the soil in bulk or as a dried product. Concentrated liquid seaweed feeds are also available.

Secateurs A modified form of scissors used mainly for pruning. There are many designs but most fall into one of two categories; those that cut with a scissor or guillotine action, and those that cut using an anvil action (where there is just one blade which comes into contact with a broader base plate).

Scissor action secateurs can cut thicker branches and produce the cleanest cut allowing fewer points of entry for pests and diseases.

It is worth spending as much as you can afford on a good pair of secateurs as the better quality ones last longer, are easier and more pleasant to use, and can be serviced regularly by the manufacturer.

Secondary branches Smaller branches developing from the primary branch.

Seed The result of sexual reproduction in plants. The actual seed is the fertilized and ripened ovule. An embryonic plant.

Seed bed An area of ground prepared specifically for the sowing of seeds. The surface soil will have been broken down into a fine tilth, the stones removed and the site levelled for even drainage.

Seed boxes / trays The traditional seed box was made of wood and measured $14\frac{1}{2}$ in by $8\frac{1}{2}$ in by 3in (36cm x 20cm x 7.5cm). Very often old kipper boxes were used as an alternative. Now, with the advent of plastics and polystyrene, seed boxes are referred to as trays and come in a multitude of colours and designs. However the traditional seed tray now measures approximately the metric equivalent of those original wooden boxes.

Ideal for raising seeds, they should be thoroughly cleaned before use to prevent the passing on of pests and diseases. Because the trays are relatively shallow young plants should be potted up fairly promptly as nutrients will soon be in short supply. Most annual bedding is sold in seedtrays or polystyrene modules.

Seed compost A range of growing composts that are specifically formulated for seed sowing. Often sold as 'seed and cutting compost' they contain lower levels of fertilizer and plant nutrients which would otherwise scorch the young roots. It is therefore necessary to pot on seedlings and cuttings at the earliest opportunity, otherwise they will become weak and straggly.

Seed drill A term used to describe the shallow furrows that seeds are sown in. Usually made with a stick or the point of a hoe, they should be as straight as possible (so it is easier to distinguish between desired seedlings and weed seedlings after germination) and of an even depth to ensure even germination along the row. A garden line or piece of wood can serve as a useful guide. Different seeds require different depths and adequate instructions are always given by suppliers on their seed packets.

Seed leaf The first leaf or leaves produced by a seed when it germinates. These may not be true leaves, and are also referred to as cotyledons.

Seedling A term which refers to young plants that have been raised from seed.

It is also a term used to describe any plant that has been raised from seed as opposed to one that has been raised by vegetative means, such as from a cutting. Such plants are valuable to the breeder as they exhibit a range of characteristics that may not be shown by the original parent plant. However, they are of limited value to the amateur gardener. An apple raised from seed will in no way bear any resemblance to the parent tree and more often than not it will be of only limited value as a cropping plant.

Seed pan Any shallow container used to germinate seeds which will be potted on before they produce an extensive root system.

Seed sower A range of gadgets sold to make sowing seeds quicker, easier and more accurate. Some are hand held, others are designed to be pushed along the soil dispensing the seeds into a prepared drill.

Selection A form of a particular plant that has been propagated vegetatively to retain its unique characteristics which are different from its parent(s).

Selective weedkiller A herbicide that can be used to target specific plants – such as broad-leaved weeds on the lawn, but which will leave other plants within the treatment area unaffected.

Self A term that is used by growers to describe a flower that has only one colour throughout.

Self-fertile A flower that can be pollinated by its own pollen, or pollen produced by flowers on the same plant.

Self-sterile A plant that cannot pollinate itself and needs a partner for fertilization.

Semi-double A term which is used to describe any flower that has more than the normal number of petals but which is not fully double.

Semi-evergreen A term used to describe a plant that is almost evergreen but which exhibits some annual leaf fall associated with a change in temperature. It can also be used to describe plants which would normally be deciduous but remain evergreen in favoured climates.

Seminal Literally means 'by seed' so the term refers to any means of propagation involving seed.

Shears 145

Sepal One section of the calyx – the outermost part of the flower. Sometimes the sepals resemble petals, and in a few instances (anemones and clematis) they actually replace them. More usually they are green or brown and protect the flower bud before it opens.

Sepaloid Resembling a sepal.

Septum A division in the ovary of a plant.

Sequestrene An organic formulation that can be applied to the soil to correct certain mineral deficiencies – particularly that of iron.

Also known as chelated iron.

Serpentine layering An interesting method of propagation whereby a number of new plants can be produced by layering one shoot several times along its length. Long shoots are pegged to the ground at intervals, each time at a node or leaf joint. Wounding at each point and the application of a rooting hormone will encourage more successful results. Clematis can easily be increased this way and plants layered in one year will be ready for lifting the following summer.

Serrated Leaves and petals that are notched or toothed along their edge.

Sessile Botanical term describing flowers and leaves that have no stalk or petiole.

Set A term which can be used to describe the process of planting out – to 'set' out bedding plants.

It can refer to tubers (potatoes), onions and shallots that are used for planting.

Also refers to blossom which has been fertilized and is developing into fruit or seed.

Setose Densely covered with sharply pointed bristles.

Shade Plants differ enormously in their light requirements. Although all plants (apart from fungi which contain no chlorophyll and therefore do not photosynthesize) require light, depending on their native habitat some require more than others. Shade is often treated as a problem when, in fact, it can be a benefit. There are vast numbers of plants from woodland situations that are excellent garden plants.

Plants that do require maximum light and which are positioned in the shade will become drawn and leggy, stop flowering and will generally look miserable.

Shanking A disorder of grapes where the stems to each individual grape wither causing the grape itself to dry up. This is usually caused by poor soil conditions or by waterlogging.

Shears Somewhat similar in appearance to a large pair of scissors, these are two handed tools used for cutting long grass, hedges, etc. There is a variety of short- and long-handled designs available all with specific uses. The average gardener could make do with one pair for trimming hedges, long grass and lawn edges (assuming that there is no powered hedgetrimmer, trimmer or lawn edging attachment on the mower available).

A sharp pair of shears is much easier to use than a blunt pair although the sharpening process is a skilled job and therefore best left to the professionals.

Sheathing A botanical term used to describe the base of a leaf which forms a tube around the stem.

Shelter belt Many plants and crops benefit from protection from extreme weather. This is particularly true in seaside locations where salt-laden wind and rain can have a devastating effect on young growth, flowers and fruit. In the garden, shelter can be provided in a number of ways: a greenhouse, frame or cloche, temporary windbreaks or a dense planting of shrubs and small trees which is commonly called a 'shelter belt'.

Shingle Stones that have been worn smooth by the action of other stones. Sometimes used to surface areas of the garden but not suitable for paths as it is difficult to compact and heavy going to walk on.

Shoddy With various waste products coming back into vogue, shoddy is making a reappearance in composts, mulches and as a moss substitute for lining hanging baskets. A by-product of the fabric industry it consists of waste fragments of wool and woollen products. It decays slowly and can be used as a bulky organic manure providing valuable humus and small amounts of nitrogen.

Short-day All plants respond to the seasons in some way and are influenced by differences in temperature, rainfall and daylight. As far as light levels are concerned, strictly speaking plants are actually responding to the length of darkness, and plants that are triggered into flower by long periods of dark are termed 'short-day'. The chrysanthemum is a good example and commercial growers go to great lengths and expense to fool the plants into thinking they are experiencing long nights all year round. In this way they can produce a good crop of flowers throughout the year.

Shot-hole disease Leaves which appear to have had small holes punched out of them. In cherries and plums it is a symptom of bacterial canker, while with peaches it is a sign of a fungal disease.

Shovel Similar in construction to a spade but with a thinner blade that is often turned up at the sides. Used for scooping up loose material such as compost, gravel, coal or soil. A London shovel has a square end, a navvy's shovel is rounded. The handle may be straight or have a D-shaped hand grip.

Shrub A plant with woody stems. Usually used to describe many-stemmed plants. Those with one woody stem are referred to as trees. However there is no real difference between large shrubs and small trees.

Shrubbery This is a term that has been largely replaced by the more modern phrase 'shrub border'. In Victorian times shrubbery was used to describe areas planted entirely with shrubs that tended to be rather boring evergreens. The areas were therefore rather dull, shady and uninteresting.

Shrublet A small shrub or woody based plant. A dwarf form.

Sickle A bladed tool used for reaping rough grass and weeds. A curved blade is attached to a short handle. Sweeping movements level and close to the ground cut the weeds and grass. For safety a hooked stick was often used in the other hand to pull debris out of the way while the sickle was still being swung.

Side dressing An application of fertilizer or mulch applied along a row of plants but not actually coming into contact with the plant itself.

Side shoot Lateral growth coming from the main stem.

Sieve A tool that is used for preparing soils for potting. Soil is pushed through a mesh which may be fine or coarse depending on the desired result. The mesh will remove stone and debris that is larger than the mesh size. In use the soil should be pushed through the mesh to make sure that valuable fibrous material isn't lost. Finer meshes will produce composts suitable for seed sowing, or can be used to produce a fine coating layer of compost, or sand, over seeds that have already been sown.

Sigmoid Curving one way and then the other – like the letter S.

Silt A type of soil produced by the weathering of rocks or the decomposition of material in a watercourse, pond or lake. It is made up of particles that are finer than sand but coarser than clay and is usually very fertile.

Silver leaf A disease that attacks plums, and occasionally peaches, nectarines, apricots, almonds, cherries and apples. A fungus penetrates the wood, usually through the site of physical damage or pruning cuts, and quickly kills the twig, branch and eventually the whole tree. Leaves take on a silver appearance as the upper and lower surfaces become disconnected. Affected branches should be removed as soon as possible and burned. Plums should be summer pruned when the risk of infection is smallest and wounds should be painted with a sealant.

Simple Not divided. A term used to describe leaves that are in one piece.

Single A term used to describe a flower that has its normal complement of petals.

Single digging Cultivating the soil to a depth of one spit or spade's depth. The basic method of soil preparation used to improve texture, bury weeds and incorporate organic matter.

Singling A dated term used to describe the process of thinning, where excess seedlings or fruits are carefully removed to allow the remainder to develop fully with less competition.

Sinuate A botanical term used to describe leaves that have a wavy and indented edge.

Siphonet The tube-like sucking mouth-part of an aphid that is inserted into a hole in the leaf made by the biting mouthparts.

Slasher A short bladed hook used for the rough trimming of hedges. More usually used on farms before the advent of tractor driven hedge trimming attachments.

Slip An old term used to describe a cutting – usually one that has been taken with a 'heel' of older wood.

Slitting An alternative to spiking a lawn to improve aeration is to cut slits in the turf. This process is usually carried out by machine and is called 'slitting'. Cutting through the grass shoots and roots also encourages the production of lateral shoots.

Slugs Feeding on live or decaying plant debris these are probably the gardener's main enemy. Not all are damaging, but those that are have earned the whole family an extremely bad reputation. Leaves, stems, roots, fruits and seedlings are all susceptible to attack at night, especially when the weather is mild and damp. Control can be achieved by hand picking them after dark, by trapping them or by the use of suitable chemical baits. Biological controls are also available.

Slugworms A term used to describe sawfly larvae which resemble slugs although on closer inspection they will be found to have legs. They can strip leaves of roses, cherries and pears, leaving the skeleton of veins, and range in colour from yellow to black. A suitable insecticide will provide effective treatment.

Smith period Period after rainfall at specific temperatures causing humid conditions that can lead to scab infection of apples.

Smokes Effective fungicide and insecticide treatment can be achieved in the glasshouse using fumigant smokes. As with all chemicals, especially ones that are so pervasive, it is essential to read the instructions carefully before use – and follow them to the letter. Plants susceptible to damage should be removed first and the glasshouse sealed thoroughly.

Smut A fungal disease of onions that affects the leaves making them look like they have been sprinkled with soot.

Snails Often accused of great garden crimes along with slugs, the effects of feeding snails are similar and the control methods the same. Snails like to hide in garden debris, under stones and on ivy-clad walls during the day. Good garden hygiene is essential to eliminate as many hiding places as possible.

Snag A stump or torn piece of wood left after careless pruning which, apart from looking unsightly, can be an introduction point for pests and disease.

Snout beetle A group of beetles which have characteristic snouts. The most commonly seen is the vine weevil although there are other species.

Soakaway A pit, that is usually filled with stones and rubble, used to collect water from a drainage system. The water fills the 'soakaway' and then gradually seeps into the subsoil.

Soboliferous A term used to describe plants that are clump-forming or produce a mass of suckers from below ground.

Sod An alternative name for an individual piece of turf.

Sod–lifter An alternative name for a turfing iron – a flat spade used to under-cut and lift turf.

Soft fruit A general term used to describe fruits that are small, stoneless and grow on low bushes (as opposed to trees). Also known as 'bush fruit', currants and raspberries are good examples.

Soft rot A disease that attacks the roots and stems of crops such as celery, cabbages, onions and some ornamentals. Bacteria attack the roots causing them to become wet and slimy, quickly resulting in the collapse and death of the whole plant. Point of entry is usually the result of damage by careless handling or hoeing. Can also affect roots, such as carrots, while they are in store.

Softwood cutting A cutting prepared from young new growth that hasn't yet produced any woody tissue. As the growth is so young, softwood cuttings need to be kept warm and moist until they have rooted.

Soil Different areas have different soils according to their geographic location and historical record. For gardeners the soil is classified in a number of ways:

It may be described as light, medium or heavy according to the proportion of sand and clay that it contains. Light soils will have a higher proportion of sand and are therefore easier to work and make free draining. Heavy soils will have a higher clay content, are heavier to work, contain more nutrients and are more moisture-retentive.

Soil may be described as acid or alkaline according to the pH value. Different plants require different pH values for optimum growth although the middle or 'neutral' range covers the vast majority of soil types and plant type is not critical.

They may be described as coarse or fine according to their texture, organic or mineral according to the humus or fibrous material content.

Generally, the ideal soil for a garden is a medium loam with a pH of about 6.5, a good supply of humus and free draining. Needless to say, very few gardeners would consider they have the perfect soil, but by careful soil management and regular cultivation it is possible to amend the soil over a number of years to be as near to ideal as possible. Additional fertilizers can also be used to correct any nutrient deficiencies.

Soil blocks Compressed cubes of compost used as individual planting modules. Used extensively in commercial horticulture, they eliminate the need for a pot and are easier to handle and avoid root disturbance when potting on or planting out.

Soil-borne A term used to describe a disease that lives in and is transmitted by the soil.

Soil capacity Different types of soil can hold different amounts of water and the actual amount they can hold without becoming waterlogged is referred to as the 'soil capacity'.

Soil conditioner Anything that is added to the soil to improve its structure. This usually takes the form of bulky organic matter with a high fibre content to open up the soil and to increase its moisture holding capacity.

There are also seaweed-derived substances called 'alginates' that bind together the very fine soil particles that are found in heavy soils.

Soilless cultivation A cultivation method that relies on the correct balance of nutrients being supplied to the plants in liquid form and the support provided by an inert growing medium such as rockwool, gravel or expanded clay granules. Used commercially for economic crops where precise control over feed levels is important, it is now beginning to enter the amateur market with 'hydroponic' systems being developed for house plants and some greenhouse crops.

Soil mark The mark left on a stem indicating the level of the soil before it was moved or transplanted.

Soil moisture deficit A term used to quantify the amount of water needed to bring a soil back to capacity.

Soil testing A valuable practice whereby the nature of a soil can be more fully understood. By testing the nutrient levels, pH, structure, etc, it is easier to understand what cultivations and additions will benefit the plants most. Kits are available for the amateur gardener or professional testing can be carried out by a number of organizations.

Soil warming The roots of plants respond well to additional heat early in the season. One way of providing this is by warming the soil with electric cables, hot water pipes or even a bed of rotting manure.

Soot Once widely available as a by-product, domestic soot was high in sulphate of ammonia and was therefore a good source of nitrogen. It also darkened the soil making it absorb more heat and therefore warm up more quickly at the beginning of the growing season. Usually stored for 3-4 months to allow excess sulphur to dissipate and then used as a soil dressing and hoed in.

Sooty mould A black mould which resembles a covering of soot found on the leaves of some shrubs. Usually a secondary infection as the sooty mould grows on honeydew – excreted by aphids on the same plant or from a tree above. The sooty mould can be carefully wiped off by hand with a sponge and soapy water. Although it doesn't damage the leaf, it prevents photosynthesis.

Sour If a soil or compost is poorly drained and has turned acid it is said to be 'sour'.

Sow The action of planting seeds either in drills, or by scattering ('broadcast').

Spade An essential tool for any gardener and one on which it is worth spending as much as possible, as a good spade should last many years. Cheap alternatives are uncomfortable to use and will probably break or bend if subjected to any force or pressure.

Used for soil cultivation and planting, there are many designs and handle permutations. There are models that are spring loaded for use by the elderly or infirm and there are special narrow bladed versions for digging narrow trenches.

Look for a spade with a tread on the top edge to prevent damage to footwear.

Spading fork A large fork with broader tines that is used for lifting root crops such as potatoes. The broader tines do less damage to the crop and mean that smaller tubers do not get missed.

Spadix Part of a special type of flower-spike. Lords and ladies (*Arum maculatum*) is a good example and the finger-like centre to the flower is the spadix. The bract that surrounds the flower is the spathe and in plants such as anthurium, it can be brightly coloured to attract pollinating insects.

Spatulate Literally meaning spatula-shaped and used to describe leaves and petals that are rounded at one end and narrow abruptly at the other.

Spawn A term used to describe the way some plants reproduce themselves. It is most often used to refer to the thread-like mycelium of mushrooms, but can equally be used to describe the small cormlets that form around the outside of gladioli corms or bulblets around other bulbous plants.

Species A botanical term used to group plants that have the same general characteristics and are able to interbreed.

Specimen plant This term refers to a plant that is grown especially to be viewed from all sides.

Sphagnum moss A particular type of moss found in moist boggy situations that can absorb vast amounts of water. Originally used as a packing material for cut flowers it became popular as a lining material for hanging baskets and was finely chopped and added to composts. It also has some antiseptic qualities.

Moss or sphagnum peat is excavated from sphagnum bogs which take many hundreds of years to regenerate.

Spicate A term used to describe something that is spike-like.

Spike Generally used to describe any flowerhead that is tall and pointed, but more correctly describes a flowerhead where the individual flowers come directly from the main stem. A good example is verbascum.

A 'spikelet' is a botanical term used to describe the flowers belonging specifically to grasses.

Spiling A way of producing top-quality root crops on poor soils. A series of deep cone-shaped holes are made in the ground with an iron bar. Each is filled with fertile sieved soil. A seed or seedling is planted at each station and the tap root develops and grows easily down through the sieved soil. Resulting roots (such as carrots and parsnips) are longer and straighter than if they had been grown in ordinary soil.

Spine Great confusion surrounds the words spine, thorn and prickle.

Thorns are technically modified branches arising from the woody part of the plant and are usually regularly placed.

Prickles are outgrowths from the outer layer of the plant, irregularly spaced which can be removed without causing any damage to the plant.

The word spine is used as a general term to describe any spiky growth.

The 'spines' of cacti are more correctly thorns. Similarly the 'thorns' of roses are technically prickles.

Although usually associated with some form of natural protection (from grazing animals), such structures are really more concerned with water conservation, as most plants grow naturally in arid conditions.

Spit Meaning a spade or fork's depth of soil. This gives the terms 'single digging' referring to the fact that the soil is cultivated to one spade or fork's depth, and 'double digging' where the cultivation is twice as deep as this.

Spittle bug An American term for a froghopper that produces its characteristic 'cuckoo-spit'.

Splice graft Simplest method of grafting a selected species onto a rootstock using matched diagonal cuts through the stems.

Spore The equivalent to seeds in lower plants, such as ferns, mosses and fungi. Being dust-like they are transported by water or air and are carried great distances by the wind.

Sport A plant that differs from the norm but which has not been raised from seed. The genetic term for such a variation is 'mutation'.

Some plants are particularly prone to producing sports which occur quite spontaneously. Chrysanthemums are a good example. Sporting is the result of a change in the character of one or more genes on the chromosomes. If this change occurs at a growing point, the new shoot or flower will have a different appearance from the rest of the plant. This shoot can then often be propagated vegetatively to produce a new plant.

Spot treatment Treatment of weeds on an individual basis – where a broader application is impossible or undesirable.

Sprain Dark streaks found in potato tubers which are the result of a physiological disorder – usually associated with fluctuations in soil water content. Can be overcome with improved drainage and cultivation techniques.

Spray This term can be used to refer to a flower stem that carries a number of flowers.

Alternatively it refers to a fine stream of droplets. Sprays of water can be used to increase the water content of plant cells that are showing distinct signs of wilting. Sprays can also be used to apply liquid feeds, insecticides and fungicides directly to the surface of the leaves where their action is instant and therefore more effective. The finer the spray, the better the coverage, and the fine droplets will also coat the undersides of the leaves so covering all areas.

A wide variety of gadgets have been designed for this kind of spraying; from the simplest hand-held hose attachment right through to hand-pumped pressurized sprayers.

Spray damage Occasionally some plants will react badly to insecticide or fungicide sprays. This is termed spray damage.

Similarly, sloppy application of herbicides can mean that spray drifts onto other areas where treatment was not needed. This may also be termed spray damage.

Spreader This term refers to a tool for spreading fertilizer over a given area. Used for the application of lawn treatments, it will deliver a preselected amount over a given area eliminating the need for careful measuring and tricky application by hand.

A spreader is also a term used to describe a substance that is added to another to allow more even distribution. Concentrated dusts are usually mixed with a spreading agent to allow better distribution. Spreaders are also added to liquids to lower the surface tension, which allows an insecticide spray to form a film over the leaf's surface.

Sprig A small twig, branch or shoot of leaves, berries or flowers.

Sprinkler This is an automatic device that is used for delivering large amounts of water to the garden, particularly to lawns which have little shade cover. May be either of an oscillating or stationary type.

Springtail A small insect that is a greenhouse pest and feeds on living and dead plant material. The insect is able to jump by means of a forked tail that is usually folded under its body. Chemical control is effective.

Sprinkle bar An attachment for a watering can used to distribute liquids at a specific rate over a given area.

Sprout Literally, a new shoot from a stem, tuber or seed.

Spud A slim-line spade used for digging out weeds. It may be long or short handled and allows minimal disturbance of the surrounding plants and soil.

Spur Referring to a twig or small branch on a tree that carries fruits (such as apples and pears). These buds multiply over the years to produce short, knobbly shoots that are covered in fruit buds. If the spurs get too large, the fruit size is reduced, so they should be pruned during the winter.

Alternatively it refers to a horned projection at the base of a flower that usually contains nectar. The best example is the flower of columbine (*Aquilegia*).

Spur bearer A fruit tree that produces its fruit on spurs, as opposed to a tip-bearing variety where the fruits are carried at the end of the previous season's growth.

Spur pruning Removal of excess lateral growth back to two or three buds to encourage fruiting spurs to form.

Stag-headed A term used to describe trees where the ends of dead branches are projecting beyond the living canopy.

Staging Benching or shelf system used in greenhouses and conservatories to maximize the use of available space. Available in a variety of shapes and designs. Modular systems give greatest flexibility, slatted tops allow better air circulation while gravel-filled trays promote a humid atmosphere.

Temporary staging (that can be dismantled) is preferable in the small greenhouse. During the winter, small plants, seedlings and cuttings can be housed at a convenient height for cultivation. The staging can then be removed when tomatoes, carnations and larger plants are being grown from late spring to mid-autumn.

Stake Many plants require additional support either because, as a result of plant breeding, they have lost their ability to support themselves, or because they are being grown in an unnatural environment. Specimen trees are a good example; if they were being grown among other trees, they would be afforded some natural protection from damage by winds.

Any form of support should be strong enough to be effective. A weak support will soon fail and can itself cause damage. It should also be as inconspicuous as possible. Herbaceous plants will soon grow through their supports and hide them effectively. Trees and shrubs are not so obliging, so a neat job is important.

Stalk Commonly but incorrectly used to describe a leaf or flower stem. A leaf stalk is a petiole; a flower stalk a pedicel. Stems can produce buds, stalks cannot.

Stamen Part of the flower that produces pollen composed of the anther (at the tip) and the filament (which attaches it to the base of the flower). This is the male organ and the pollen fertilizes the ovary of the flower. In some flowers the stamens resemble petals – the case with many double and semi-double blooms.

Staminode This term refers to a stamen that produces no pollen and is therefore infertile. Staminodes sometimes resemble petals, as in some peonies.

Stand A term used to describe a group of plants growing in one area in isolation.

Also, a group of trees or shrubs.

Standard Botanically, this term refers to the upper petal of flowers belonging to the pea family (*Leguminosae*).

It is also used to describe the broad, upright petals of some irises.

In gardening, the term refers to trees or shrubs that have a bare main stem. The branches or sideshoots have fallen naturally or have been removed to create an artificial standard (as with standard fuchsias). Some trees and shrubs are actually even grafted onto bare main stems to create standard forms. Roses and the Kilmarnock willow are excellent examples of this.

'Half-standard' refers to standard plants that are on shorter stems – around 1m (3ft) in height.

Starting The process of encouraging dormant plants to come into growth, usually after their resting period, by providing optimum growing conditions (warmth, light and moisture).

Steeping This can refer to the production of a liquid manure by suspending a bag of animal manure in a bucket of water and using the fluid as a liquid feed.

It can also refer to the process of soaking seeds which have a very hard seed coat that may not be broken down sufficiently or quickly enough by the available soil moisture.

Stele The central core of vascular plants.

Stellate Star-like, with branches radiating from one central point. Also used to describe flowers that are star-shaped, and may be Latinized and used in a plant name such as *Magnolia stellata*.

Stem In its broadest sense this describes the main part of a plant that appears above ground level from which buds will develop.

More often it is used to describe a small branch or petiole that supports a leaf, flower or fruit.

Stem cutting A cutting prepared from a stem.

Stem-rooting A term used to describe a plant characteristic where roots are produced above ground.

Stem rot General term describing a range of diseases that attack the stems of plants.

Stepover A term used to describe a single tiered espalier fruit tree. Little more than 30cm (1ft) high, 'stepover' trees are a very effective – and productive – way of edging beds and borders. They are easy to maintain and can produce a good crop of top quality fruit each year.

Sterile A term used to describe any plant or flower that is incapable of reproduction.

A plant that is self-sterile is incapable of pollinating itself. This is of great importance with economic crops, such as apples, pears and cherries, where suitable pollinators also have to be planted with certain varieties.

Sterilization Usually associated with a soil treatment to destroy weed seeds, insects and fungal spores. The term is misleading as it is only a partial process – some bacteria are beneficial to the soil.

Can be carried out using heat (derived from hot water, steam or by baking) or with chemicals.

Stigma The tip of the pistil or female part of the flower. It is often sticky so that pollen sticks to the end when it is ready for fertilization.

Stilt-roots Adventitious roots that support the plant. This is a feature of mangrove swamps and plants that grow in warm coastal regions.

Stipule A leaf-like structure growing from the base of a leaf-stalk or petiole. They usually appear in pairs and are soon shed as the leaf develops.

Stock The root portion of a grafted plant, or plants being grown specifically for their roots with a view to grafting. The term 'stock' can also be used to describe a plant that is kept purely for vegetative propagation purposes.

Stolon A shoot that runs level with the soil producing roots and shoots. Strawberry runners are a good example.

Stomata These are the tiny microscopic pores found on the undersides of leaves. They control the water content of the plant by opening to allow evaporation and closing to prevent it. *Singular Stoma*

Stone Botanically this refers to the seed of many members of the *Prunus* family; such as plums, cherries, apricots, peaches and nectarines. *Sm*

Stool This term generally refers to an old plant that is being used to produce propagation material. Lifted chrysanthemums are a good example of this and are usually encouraged to produce strong new shoots. These are taken as cuttings and the parent plant or 'stool' is then discarded once it has been used.

Stopping In order to encourage a plant to make sideshoots it is necessary to remove the fastest growing tip. This process is termed stopping. With crops such as carnations and chrysanthemums it will encourage more sideshoots and therefore more flowers. This process extends the productive life of plants and can be used to time crops more efficiently.

Storage organs A term which is used to describe specialized plant organs that are used to store food and fluid during periods of dormancy. The most common are bulbs, tubers, corms and rhizomes, although the term applies equally to organs above ground, such as the thick fleshy stems of some cacti.

Storage rot This term can refer to any disease that attacks stored fruit and vegetables – normally infecting damaged or bruised tissues.

Stove/Stove house Refers to a greenhouse where a high temperature – 21-24°C (70-75°F) – is maintained throughout the year, with equally high humidity levels. Used to grow exotic plants, the name is probably derived from the original method of heating such structures.

Strain Even named varieties of plants raised from seed tend to vary slightly. Although seed companies take great care when selecting seed of particular varieties, some variation is inevitable and can increase with subsequent generations. Seed that is perpetuated by different companies that originally came from the same source can therefore be markedly different several generations later. Such seed is then referred to as a strain, and if the difference becomes more marked, the plants may then be listed as 'forms'.

Strap-shaped This is a botanical term which is used to describe leaves that are long and thin but have predominantly parallel sides.

Stratification In the wild, seeds receive a period of cold during the winter months. This is sometimes necessary to break dormancy and encourage germination and if the process is mimicked artificially by the gardener, it is known as 'stratification'. Tree and shrub seeds are most commonly treated in this way.

Seeds are placed between layers of sand in pots or seed trays and placed in an exposed position in the garden. Left there during the winter throughout periods of frost, freezing and thawing the seeds are then sown in spring and will germinate much more readily.

Stratification can also be carried out in a domestic refrigerator.

Straw Soil conditioner; stems of wheat, barley and oats add valuable fibre and improve the aeration of impoverished soils. When you are digging in, thoroughly mix in the straw to help decay, although fresh straw can take nitrogen from the soil. If composted first this is not a problem.

Fresh straw is useful as a protective mulch; around strawberries to prevent the fruits being splashed with mud, and over less hardy perennials and shrubs like a thick insulating quilt.

Strawberry pot A specialized container (originally terracotta, but now more usually plastic) with holes around the sides in which strawberry plants are grown. The idea is to maximize the yield from a relatively small area and give the gardener greater control over watering, protection and harvesting. Fruits are kept off the ground so there is also no need to mulch. Strawberry pots are a good decorative option for adding to the small but productive garden.

Streak A name given to various virus diseases which manifest themselves as brown or blackish spots and streaks on the flowers, leaves, fruits and stems of affected plants. Tomatoes and sweet peas are sometimes affected and the plants become weak, eventually dying.

As with other virus diseases it can be spread by sucking insects (such as aphids) or by human intervention with contaminated pruning knives and secateurs.

Striate A term describing the pattern of a leaf where the stripes, ribs or grooves are longitudinal.

Strig Refers to a cluster of fruit including the main stem and stalks. Clusters of fruit found on blackcurrants are a good example. The action of removing the fruits from these clusters and from their stalks is called 'strigging'.

Strike This term refers to the rooting of a cutting – 'to strike a cutting'.

A strike is also equivalent to two bushels (an obsolete dry measurement).

Strigose This is a term used to describe leaves or stems that are covered in stiff bristles or hairs.

Strip cropping Harvesting the whole crop in one go rather than picking it over periodically. Can also refer to the growing of crops in rows so they can be more easily protected with cloches.

Strobilus This is in fact another name for a cone produced by conifers. Hops are a good but less common example.

Stub The stump of a tree left after felling, or a piece of branch or twig that remains on the branch after pruning.

Stunt Anything that slows down the growth and eventual size of a plant is said to 'stunt' it. The cause may be lack of water or nutrients, chemical damage, lack of light or exposure to extreme weather.

Style The central part of the pistil or female part of a flower. The style joins the stigma (the sticky pollen-receptive end) to the ovary (where the seeds will form).

Sub-alpine A plant that originates from the lower slopes of alpine regions that will happily grow on higher slopes but below the tree line.

Sub-shrub A plant that produces some woody mature growth but the soft growth of which will die down in winter.

Sub-soil The soil layer that lies beneath and is markedly different from the surface (or top) soil. The nature and character of the sub-soil will differ from one area to another, depending on the geography of the land. The character of the sub-soil will influence that of the topsoil lying over it. Thus if the sub-soil is clay, the surface soil is more likely to become waterlogged.

Deep cultivations, such as trenching and double digging, are a good way of improving the sub-soil.

Subterranean Describing the parts of a plant that are found underground.

Sub-tropical Used to describe any plant that originates from areas bordering the tropical geographical zones of the world. Susceptible to frost, sub-tropical plants can be grown in temperate climates as long as winter protection is given.

Subulate This is a botanical term which is used to describe any leaves that are long, narrow and taper to a point.

Successional A process of periodic sowing of vegetable and flower crops so that they mature over a longer period giving a continuous supply.

Succulent This term can be used to refer to any plant that has modified itself to cope with drought conditions. Cacti are one example.

Leaves and/or stems have been modified to help store water and reduce water loss through transpiration. Succulents need to replenish their water reserves and would normally do so during the heavy desert rains.

Sucker Refers to growths that come directly from the rootstock of a plant. These should be removed as they will have the characteristics of the rootstock rather than the selected variety that has been grafted or budded above. They are also usually more vigorous and will have an adverse effect on the health and vigour of the selected variety.

Suckers should be removed cleanly from the root – any vestige of growth left will develop buds and regrow. Some gardeners recommend pulling them off the roots by hand.

The term sucker also refers to the adventitious growth some plants make from their own roots. These can be a nuisance and they are usually dug out, but it can also be a useful means of propagation. Raspberry canes can be lifted and increased in this way.

Sulphate of ammonia A nitrogen-rich soluble chemical fertilizer. Being soluble it is quick-acting and ideal for a boost of growth in spring and summer. It must not touch the leaves or they will be scorched. Can also be used as a soil conditioner to lower the pH levels.

Also the main ingredient of lawn sand used to feed the turf and destroy broad-leaved weeds.

Sulphate of copper A compound used as a winter fungicide but extremely caustic to foliage so needs careful application. When mixed with lime it is called 'Bordeaux mixture' – a popular fungicide.

Sulphate of magnesium Magnesium deficiency shows as a yellowing of the leaves and can be corrected by an application of Epsom Salts (sulphate of magnesium) in dry form sprinkled on the soil or in solution as a foliar feed.

Sulphate of potash A valuable potash-rich fertilizer that is readily soluble and therefore quick acting. Can be used as a tonic to cure potassium deficiency which manifests itself as a bluing or yellowing of the leaves and browning at the tips.

Sulphur In powder form is an effective and natural fungicide which can be applied as a dust so there is no increase in humidity (which would aggravate an existing fungal problem in a greenhouse).

Sulphur is also a 'trace element' – necessary, but in small doses, for healthy plant growth.

Summer chafer Large beetles often seen flying on warm summer evenings. The adult beetle and larvae eat holes into leaves and roots.

Summer pruning Any pruning that is carried out in the summer months. It is usually carried out to check the vigour of new growth and channel more energy into producing more flower buds or developing fruits.

Sundial Now treated as an attractive garden ornament, sundials were originally the only way of telling the time. The arm that casts the shadow on the base plate is called the 'gnomon'.

Superphosphate of lime A 'base dressing' used prior to planting, superphosphate of lime is rich in phosphates and, despite having the word lime in its name, will not affect the soil's pH.

Support Anything which is used to hold up a plant. It may be made of canes and twigs in the vegetable garden, or stakes, trellis, pergolas or even other plants in the ornamental garden.

Surfactant A detergent that is added to certain fertilizer and insecticide sprays that breaks down the surface tension of the carrying water making it more effective at wetting the leaves and stems.

Sward A term used to refer to an area of short grass.

Swathe Refers to the width of grass cut by a mower.

Sweet When used as a gardening term it refers to soil that is either neutral or alkaline – not acid.

Swelling A term that is used to describe the process of a bud enlarging after a period of dormancy, prior to leaf and flower production.

Symbiosis A natural association between two living organisms that is beneficial to both. A good example is the nitrogen-fixing bacteria found on the roots of leguminous plants. The legumes benefit from additional nitrogen and the bacteria receive nutrients from the plants.

Symphilid This is a root-eating insect that resembles a centipede although it has only 14 body segments and 12 pairs of legs. It can be controlled using an insecticide.

Sympodial A term used to describe plants where the terminal bud forms a flower or dies and subsequent growth is carried out by the lateral buds.

Synanthous A botanical term describing leaves that appear alongside the flowers.

Synonym An alternative name for the same plant. This is usually the result of a plant being reclassified botanically, or from having been named by two different people in the first place.

Synthetic fungicide A term that describes all man-made fungicides.

Synthetic insecticide Used to refer to man-made insecticides.

Syringe A type of hand-held sprayer for applying water or pesticides. In the same way as a traditional bicycle pump, water is drawn into the barrel by drawing out the plunger and then pushed out through a nozzle at the end, forming a fine droplet spray over the plant.

Systemic A generic term for some insecticides and fungicides that are actually taken into the plant. Any organism actually feeding on the treated plant will then be affected by the pesticide. Application is therefore far more discriminating in that only the target pests are affected but care should be taken to follow manufacturers' recommended harvest intervals if used on food crops.

T

Tamping The process of firming or gently compacting the soil around a new plant, or after soil cultivation.

Tap root The main anchoring root of a plant that usually goes straight downwards into the soil. A carrot is a good example of an edible tap root.

Tar oil wash A formulation of tar distillates used to treat dormant fruit trees during the winter months. When sprayed on the twigs, branches and trunk it effectively kills overwintering aphid eggs, scale insects, caterpillars and algae. A tar oil winter wash will colour green plants brown so grass beneath and shrubs adjacent to trees being treated should also be covered.

Taxonomy The study of the structure and classification of plants and animals according to their relationships.

Temperature All plants have temperatures at which they are happiest – usually relating to their native habitats. However, plants can adapt to different temperature ranges (upper and lower levels) which is why some greenhouse-raised plants that are normally hardy have to be acclimatized (or hardened off) before being planted out in the garden.

Excessively high temperatures are as damaging as extremely low ones. High temperatures lead to excessive transpiration and consequent water loss and wilting. Low temperatures slow down the flow of sap and can even cause physical damage to the plant cells if freezing occurs.

Tender A rather loose term used to describe a plant's inability to cope with cold temperatures and frost. Susceptibility also varies according to the maturity of growth; young leaves and shoots with the highest moisture content are the most tender.

Tender annual A plant that germinates, flowers and produces seed in one year, but which requires glasshouse protection for the whole of its life cycle.

Tendril Modified leaves, leaflets or shoots that help a plant to climb by twining and coiling around adjacent supports.

Tepal The term that describes parts of a flower where there is no differentiation between the sepals and petals. A magnolia flower is a good example.

Terete A word used to describe the stem of a plant that is cylindrical and smooth.

Terminal Used to describe the top leaf, bud, branch, flower or shoot of a plant – usually the most vigorous growing point.

Ternate A term used to describe something that can be subdivided evenly into three. A clover leaf is a good example of a ternate leaf form.

Terrarium A development of the 'Wardian case', a terrarium is an enclosed growing environment, usually made of glass and resembling a miniature glasshouse. Now also made of transparent plastic, a terrarium is useful for growing and displaying house plants that like a warm, humid atmosphere. Care should be taken with the amount of watering as there is no drainage, but as the plants are growing in a closed environment water lost through transpiration will condense on the sides of the terrarium and run down, back into the growing medium.

Terrestrial Meaning 'of the ground' the term is used botanically to describe plants that grow in compost rather than on rock, in water or on other plants.

Tessellated A term used to describe the chequer-board patterning found on some flowers or leaves. The snake's head fritillary (*Fritillaria meleagris*) is a good example of a flower with tessellated petals.

Testa This refers to the outer covering of a seed; the seedcoat.

Tetraploid A genetic term for a plant that has twice the number of chromosomes that are normal for that species. They are often more vigorous than plants carrying the normal number of chromosomes.

Thallophyte The lowest form of life in the plant kingdom – fungi, bacteria, etc. The main body of the plant is a 'thallus'.

Thallus Vegetative growth that has not developed distinct roots, shoots or leaves.

Thatch A layer of dead organic matter in a lawn that hinders the penetration of water and nutrients to the roots below. Removed by raking or 'scarifying'.

Thermometer An instrument for measuring air and soil temperatures and of great value to the gardener. Temperatures may be measured in Celsius (°C) or Fahrenheit (°F).

To measure the temperature range over a given period a maximum/minimum thermometer is useful, as it records the highest and lowest temperatures between periods and then it can be re-set. In recent years, electronic thermometers and those employing heat-sensitive paints have become available to the gardener and are very accurate, reliable and easy to use.

Thermostat An electrical gadget used for regulating the operating temperature of heating systems. In the glasshouse, a thermostatically controlled heater will operate only when required, thus saving energy and time.

Thimble An obsolete term that was used to describe the smallest available flowerpot when pots were made from clay. It measured 5cm (2in) across the top and stood just 5cm (2in) high.

Thinning The removal of excess seedlings and plants allowing those that remain a better chance of reaching maturity or maximum potential.

The term can also be applied to the removal of unwanted flowers and young fruits – again to ensure that those remaining reach maximum potential.

It is often a good idea to thin plants twice, removing only half the excess at the first stage. Then if there are casualties after the first thinning there are plenty of nearby replacements to choose from.

Thiram A fungicide that can be used in powdered form on soil to protect seedlings from soil-borne diseases, or mixed with water as a fungicidal drench.

Thrips A group of insects that suck the sap from the leaves, stems and flowers of a wide range of plants causing brown or silver spotting and streaking. Insects vary in colour from yellow through to black and are most active in warm, dry weather. Because they are associated with warm, sultry weather they have the common name of 'thunderflies'. Maintaining high humidity and use of a suitable insecticide will offer some control.

Throat This refers to the narrowest part of a tubular flower.

Thumb Second smallest size of clay flowerpot measuring 6cm (2$\frac{1}{2}$in) wide at the top and standing 6cm (2$\frac{1}{2}$in) high.

Tie In gardening terms, anything used to attach a plant to its support.

Till The process of soil cultivation.

Tillering This term describes the production of vigorous lateral shoots from the base of a plant. Tillering can be encouraged in various ways, most notably in lawn grasses through scarifying, raking or slitting.

Tilth A good, crumbly soil structure produced by careful cultivation and soil improvement. A fine 'tilth' will be level and free of large lumps of soil and stones – ideal for sowing seeds. Tilth depends on the nature of the soil and the way in which it is cultivated.

Tines A term that refers to the individual prongs of garden tools such as forks, rakes and aerators. In the case of lawn aerators the tines may be hollow so they remove a core of soil.

Tip bearer A term used to describe some fruit trees that bear fruit buds at the ends of their shoots.

Tip cutting A stem cutting taken from the top of a (non-flowering) shoot.

Tip layering A method of vegetative propagation used on some plants that produce long, bendable shoots. The blackberry is a good example. The shoots are bent towards the ground and the tip pegged down to the soil. If the soil is kept moist during the winter, the tip will produce roots and can be separated from the parent plant the following spring.

Tissue culture A form of vegetative propagation where minute pieces of plant are grown on a special nutrient gel under sterile laboratory conditions.

Toadstool A term used to describe the fruiting bodies of some fungi such as mushrooms. Some are highly poisonous.

Tomentose Term describing a plant that is covered in short, closely matted hairs.

Toothed A term used to describe a tooth-like edging of petals or leaves.

Top cutting A stem cutting made from the top shoot of a plant.

Top-dressing Applications which are made to the surface of the soil and left there (rather than being dug or hoed in). May be the application of fertilizers or bulky organic materials (although surface applications of the latter are usually referred to as 'mulches').

Top fruit Any form of fruit that has come from a tree rather than a bush. Apples and pears are the most common examples.

Topiary At its height in the seventeenth century, this term refers to the clipping of trees, shrubs and ornamental plant into fanciful shapes and designs. Now becoming more popular again using evergreen plants such as yew, box and ivy. The latter is usually grown over a 'topiary frame' – a wirework support in the shape of the desired creation.

Topsoil The uppermost layer of soil that is usually the most fertile and in which most cultivation is carried out. Only larger shrubs and trees penetrate to the 'sub-soil' beneath.

Topping The removal of the growing point of a plant for any reason other than to promote sideshoots. Thus, hedging plants that have reached the desired height are 'topped', as are broad bean plants to prevent the soft, succulent tops attracting blackfly.

Top-working This is a way of rejuvenating fruit trees whereby the main branches are cut down but the stump is used as a stock for grafting. The process of producing 'standard' trees through grafting onto

a main stem could also be referred to as 'top-working'.

Tortuous Meaning irregularly bent in all directions. Often used as a variety name, such as with the contorted willow – *Salix babylonica* 'Tortuosa'.

Total weedkiller An extremely powerful herbicide that will kill all plant growth and should therefore be used sparingly and according to the manufacturers' recommendations. Good for clearing larger areas of land but of limited use on a domestic scale.

Toxic The same as poisonous – injurious to the health of plants and/or animals.

Trace element Plants require a vast number of nutrients in various quantities for healthy growth. Those that are required in minute amounts are termed 'trace elements'. An excess may be harmful and a deficiency will cause poor growth. Compound fertilizers contain the major nutrients and trace elements.

Trailing A term which is used to describe plants that are prostrate but do not produce roots.

Training The art of getting a plant to assume the shape you want it to by selective pruning and encouragement of chosen shoots. Badly placed shoots are often removed and selected ones encouraged in the direction the gardener wishes them to grow.

Translocation The process of moving water and nutrients around the vascular system of a plant.

Transpiration Part of the natural process of photosynthesis whereby plants lose water through their leaves into the atmosphere. Should the rate of transpiration exceed the rate of water uptake by the roots, the plant will begin to wilt.

Transplant The moving of a plant from one location to another. Most often used to refer to the process of moving young plants from the original seedbed to their final positions.

Trapeziform A term used to describe parts of a plant that are four-sided.

Tread Firming the soil with the feet so that plant roots can gain a good foothold. Treading should never be done on wet soil as the soil's structure would be severely damaged.

The term also refers to the part of a spade or fork where the foot is used to push it into the soil.

Tree A large, woody perennial plant that usually has one main stem, the trunk, which then subdivides into branches.

Trees are termed 'deciduous' if they shed their leaves during the winter, or 'evergreen' if they retain foliage throughout the year.

Tree banding Method of trapping crawling insects on a very sticky band tied around the trunk as they climb the tree to lay their eggs or hibernate.

Tree guard A protective device to prevent rabbits, deer (and humans) from damaging the trunks of newly planted trees. The guard may be wood, metal or plastic.

Tree pruners Long handled tools enabling stems and small branches to be removed from a tree without the need to climb it.

Tree surgery Any formative or repair work carried out to a tree. An operation best left to the professionals who are used to working with dangerous machines (such as chain saws) at great heights under difficult circumstances.

Trellis A criss-cross pattern of light wooden, plastic or metal battens formed into a decorative panel.

Trench A deeply dug strip of land that is intended for growing gross feeding crops such as sweet peas and runner beans. Ideal on light, free-draining soils but can often lead to problems of waterlogging on wet, clay soils.

Also ideal for growing crops that need blanching (such as celery) as the trench can be backfilled as the plants grow, keeping the stems in the dark.

Trenching A form of deep cultivation where the soil is broken up to a depth of 0.7–1m (2½–3ft).

Trichome A hair-like outgrowth from the leaf epidermis, often tipped with a secreting gland.

Trickle irrigation A method of watering whereby a small amount of water is delivered to individual plants (or rows of plants) via a perforated pipe or system of small, individual pipes linked to a reservoir. Used commercially, the system has been introduced into the amateur market as it is economical, can be automated and can also be set up to deliver precise amounts of liquid fertilizer to specific plants.

Trifoliate A botanical term used to describe leaves that are composed of three leaflets.

Trimmer A powered hand tool used for cutting grass and light vegetation. The cutter may be a nylon line or metal or plastic blade, although the latter are usually termed brushcutters as they are more robust and can tackle thicker stems. Machines may be electric or petrol driven.

Tripartite A term used to describe, petals, sepals, bracts or leaves that can be divided equally into three.

Triple cordon A 'cordon' tree that has been formed with three main stems. Some triple cordons will be composed of three different varieties which are compatible for fertilization of the flowers, all grafted onto the same rootstock.

Triploid A plant that contains three sets of chromosomes instead of the usual two. Triploid plants are usually sterile.

Tripterous A term used to describe parts of a plant (usually the stem, leaf or fruit) that has three wings.

Tristylous A term that is used to describe flowers where the styles have three distinct relative lengths.

Tropical Describes a plant that originated from the tropics.

Tropism This is the movement of a plant in response to an outside stimulus, such as light.

Trowel An essential small hand tool for every gardener used for planting, weeding etc. Modified blade shapes may be available for specific tasks. A long narrow blade, graduated with measurements, is designed for bulb planting.

True-breeding A plant that will produce seed through self-fertilization that gives rise to plants that are the same as the parent (although genetically there will be differences but these are not perceptible to the human eye).

Trug A wooden basket made from wide slats of wood held together by a wooden rim. A useful and attractive garden accessory which will last a lifetime.

Trumpet A term used to describe flowers that start narrow at the plant end and then flare out rather like the bell of a trumpet.

Truncate In its botanical sense this term refers to parts of a plant that cut off suddenly at the end (leaves that look as though the ends have been snipped off).

Trunk Most usually used to refer to the main stem of a tree.

The term can also be applied to the thickened stems of tree ferns and also to some primulas.

Truss A compact cluster of fruit or flowers at the end of a stem.

Tuber A swollen underground stem or root used by a plant to store food (usually in the form of starch). Stem tubers (such as the potato) have 'eyes', while root tubers (such as the dahlia) do not. Tubers are a useful means of propagation if

separated from the adult plant with at least one growth bud.

Tubercle A small swelling or tuber. *May be borne in leaf axils (eg. Begonia) or on roots (eg legumes)*

Tubular floret Florets typical of daisy flower centres (members of the *compositae* family) which are tubular in structure.

Tufa A very porous form of limestone (calcium carbonate), sometimes used for rock gardens and to grow alpines that prefer an alkaline environment.

Tunic The outer protective layer of a bulb or corm, usually papery in character.

Tunicated A botanical term used to describe bulbs in which the scales are wrapped around each other. Onions are one example.

Turbinate Cone shaped – narrow at the top and broader at the base.

Turf A general term used to describe the grass on a lawn and referring to the leaves, thatch, roots and soil as a whole. Turf is the easiest but most expensive way of laying a new lawn and requires careful site preparation and laying.

'Turf loam' refers to turf that has been stacked grass-side-down and composted to produce a fibrous loam for potting and general cultivation.

A turf can also be a piece of dried peat.

Turf beater A tool used to settle and level newly turfed lawns.

Turfing iron This term describes a special flattened tool used to undercut and lift turf. Its use requires some skill and has been replaced on a commercial scale by mechanical means.

Turgid A term describing something that is swollen or bloated, usually with water. When plant cells loose their 'turgidity' their structure is lost and the plant will then wilt.

Turion An underground bud that grows upwards developing into a new stem.

A detached overwintering bud of an aquatic plant or any adventitious shoot or sucker.

Twitten A narrow path that runs between two hedges or walls.

Tying An additional form of support for weak or vulnerable plants. The term 'tying-in' usually refers to climbers and vines where errant shoots are tied back to the support system.

Type A botanical term that refers to the first plant of a particular species that was used as the standard for its description. Therefore, it does not necessarily follow that the 'type' will be the commonest form found in nature.

U

Uliginous A term used to describe plants that grow in damp, boggy areas.

Umbel A botanical term describing a flower structure where the individual flower stalks join the main stem at one point. Plants that have this characteristic in common are classified as 'umbellifers', the most common example being the carrot.

Umbo A knobbly projection sometimes found on the caps of fungi.

Umbraculiferous A term which is used to describe a leaf or flower that is shaped like an umbrella.

Uncinate Meaning hooked at the end or hook-shaped.

Underplant Planting beneath a canopy of other plants. The most common and successful example is the 'underplanting' of shrubs with spring bulbs which extends the period of interest and display.

Understorey Term used to describe the plant growth that is found beneath the tree canopy.

Undulate A botanical term meaning wavy edges, and used to describe leaves and petals that display such a characteristic.

Union This refers to the join on a grafted plant where the 'stock' and 'scion' have bonded together.

Unisexual A botanical term used to describe plants that produce flowers of one sex only.

Urceolate A term referring to the urn-like appearance of a flower.

Vascular Bundle Strand of fluid-conducting tissue of which zylem and phloem are the most important constituents.
Gymnosperms/ dicotyledons- v.b.'s are arranged in a hollow cylinder in the stem; monocotyledons- v.b.'s are scattered through the stem tissue.

Vacuole A 'cavity' in the protoplasm of most plant cells filled with a water solution of sugars, salts, acids and other substances.

Variegated A term used to describe differences in coloration of leaves, stems, and sometimes in flowers.

Variegation is usually a combination of green, white and yellow coloration and the result of some cells having less green pigment (chlorophyll). The patterning may be regular (in stripes or around the leaf margins) or irregular (in blotches and random patches).

Variegated plants often arise as sports from other plants and are therefore propagated vegetatively. They are variable garden plants adding colour and interest to the border even when not in flower, although they should be contrasted with plain-leaved plants for maximum effect.

With less chlorophyll they are less vigorous and do not cope with shade or semi-shade too well.

Variety A term used in the classification of plants to identify a variation in a species that is distinct and has its own name.

Vascular A term refering to the transport system of plants whereby the water, sugars and minerals are transported between the roots and the leaves via strands of conducting tissue called 'vascular bundles'.

Vegetable A term used commonly used to describe edible parts of plants that are usually served with the main course of a meal (as opposed to fruits which are edible parts of plants served as a dessert course). However, this is not accurate in that tomatoes and marrows are botanically fruits – but on the whole the differentiation survives.

Vegetative A term used botanically to describe the part of plants that are capable of growth (in effect anything other than a flower).

Vegetative propagation Cuttings, division, grafting, layering and budding are all termed 'vegetative propagation' because they do not involve seeds. The advantage is that plants will be identical to the parents.

Plants propagated vegetatively from one parent are termed 'clones'.

...etative Reproduction Asexual reproduction ...sisting in the development of part of the plant body into a new individual.

Vein A strand of water conducting tissues visible from the surface of the stem, leaf or petal.

Velutinous A term used to describe parts of a plant that are covered with dense, fine hairs so that the surface resembles velvet.

Venation A botanical term used to describe the arrangement of the veins within a leaf.

Ventilation The circulation of air in a confined space. Ventilation is really of paramount importance in artificial growing conditions such as greenhouses, conservatories, frames, cloches and propagators. The movement of air should be sufficient to maintain optimum levels of heat and humidity. Too much and these levels will drop, too little and they will rise, in both instances having a detrimental effect on the plants within. Heat causes wilting, cold slows the rate of growth and high humidity can lead to increased problems with fungal diseases.

Managing to adjust these levels and provide the correct amount of ventilation is largely part of becoming an experienced gardener although amateurs can equip themselves with an array of gadgets to help. Making sure the greenhouse or conservatory has sufficient roof and side opening windows is a good start as many don't, and the installation of fans and automatic vent and door openers will also help.

Ventricose A term used to describe something (usually a fruit) that is swollen more on one side than the other.

Verdan A kinin.

Vermiculite A natural form of mica that curls and expands when subjected to extreme temperature. The expanded granules have remarkable water holding capacity while still remaining free draining and are therefore a useful addition to composts. Principally used for its insulating properties in the building trade it has gained acceptance in the commercial and amateur gardening market because it is light, pleasant to handle and cheap.

Vernal Appearing in spring.

Vernalization A variety of processes can be employed to fool seeds and plants into thinking that they have been through a winter. This is termed 'vernalization' and is used to trigger germination or rapid growth when sufficient light, heat and moisture are provided.

Vernation The arrangement of leaves in the bud – sometimes a useful means of identification.

Verticillium wilt A fungal disease that can affect a wide range of herbaceous plants and some shrubs and trees. The effect is a brown marking on the stems and plants often start to wilt.

Vesicle A small bladder-like sac or cavity filled with water or air.

Vessel Tube-like structure formed of elongated cells arranged end-to-end, serving as a water-conducting element of xylem.

Viable A term used to describe seed that is capable of germinating.

Vigour The ability of a plant to produce fast, healthy growth.

Vine eye A special nail used to support vines and climbing plants.

Virescence The appearance of green pigmentation in plants that would not ordinarily exhibit it.

Virus Microscopic particles that increase rapidly within the plants' cells causing a wide range of disorders – most commonly disrupting the colour and patterning of leaves and flowers.

A virus is transmitted by poor hygiene and by sap-sucking insects. The nursery trade and plant breeders propagate susceptible plants from virus-free stock.

In some plants, such as *Abutilon megapotamicum* 'Variegatum', the virus causing the blotching and mottling of the leaves is considered desirable and the character is perpetuated by vegetative propagation. However, normally plants showing infection are rogued out and then burned.

Viscid Covered in a sticky exudation.

Vista A view which is confined on either side by trees, hills or other objects. Cleverly thought out vistas can give the impression of great depth to a small garden.

Viticulture The growing of vines.

Viviparous A literal translation from the Latin meaning to produce live young; exhibited by some aphids. The process leads to a very quick increase in the population.

The term is also loosely applied by botanists to plants that produce bulbils and offsets that start to grow while they are still attached to the parent plant. A good example here is *Tolmiea menziesii* – the piggy-back plant that produces small baby plants in the centre of fully developed leaves.

Wall Brick or stone structures that fulfil two roles in the garden.

Their role may be one of division, separating the garden from neighbours or one part of the garden from another, or they may be structural in that they retain soil to create terraces or raised beds. Both require some skill in construction and good foundations (particularly in the case of retaining walls that will be supporting a vast weight of soil).

Either way they add a valuable extra dimension to the garden and afford support and protection to adjacent plants.

Specialized walls may be built by using other materials such as drystone walls (built without mortar) and turf walls (these are created by laying turfs one on top of another).

Wall nail A special type of masonry nail that can be driven into the mortar between courses of brick or stone. A flexible lead strap attached to the head can then be used to secure plant stems to the wall.

Wardian case A closed glass case designed by the plant hunter Nathaniel Ward (1791-1868) to transport rare and tender plants back to Britain aboard ship. Affording complete control over the enclosed environment the cases became fashionable in domestic situations for growing collections of ferns and orchids that relish a damp, humid atmosphere.

Wart disease A fungal disease of potatoes that causes part of the tuber to become disfigured and wart-like.

Wasps A group of stinging insects belonging to the order *Hymenoptera*, the most common of which feed on garden fruits. Nests are common in attics and under house eaves and can cause considerable nuisance. Control can be achieved using chemical fumigants and baits.

Water A colourless compound composed of two molecules of hydrogen for every one of oxygen (H_2O), and the lifeblood of the plant (and animal) kingdom. Depending on the local geography, tapwater can contain a high level of mineral salts. This can cause problems for some plants, such as lime–hating azaleas being watered with water collected from an area with underlying chalk. For this reason collecting rainwater from the roofs of buildings is best for garden use, and is absolutely essential in times of drought or where water meters are connected to the mains supply.

Water garden A term applied to gardens created around streams, pools, bog gardens and their associated plantings. They may be formal or informal. Formal gardens were very much in vogue in the seventeenth and eighteenth centuries, particularly in Italy (and Italianate gardens anywhere) and used geometric designs incorporating canals, rills, water spouts and fountains that relied more on the decorative effect of the water rather than the plants. Informal water gardens re-created a natural setting and would mimic natural pools, lakes, streams and watercourses with lush, colourful plantings of marginals and aquatics.

Watering Water is essential to all plants and its application needs careful consideration. Too much or too little will be detrimental to the plants, and gauging what they need in addition to natural rainfall is all part and parcel of being a good gardener. Greenhouse cultivation, where the plants are totally dependent on artificial watering, is probably the ultimate test of a gardener's craft.

Water itself varies depending on the geographical nature of the areas where it is collected. Various elements and salts that are naturally occurring in the soil will go into solution in water permeating through it. With plants having different likes and tolerances, using the 'wrong' water can sometimes lead to toxicity or cases of mineral deficiency.

Watering can A hand-held metal or plastic spouted container used to transport water. A 'rose' attachment may be added to the spout to produce a fine spray of droplets which are less damaging to seedlings and young plants. Watering in this way is an ideal time to feed plants using a water-soluble fertilizer.

Water shoot A vigorous shoot produced from the trunk or branch of a tree. In the case of fruit trees these are unproductive and should be removed. In all cases they can lead to a loss of vigour throughout the plant and congested growth.

Water absorbing granules Synthetic sugar-like granules that are capable of absorbing many times their own weight of water and then releasing it slowly to the surrounding soil. They are a valuable way of reducing the frequency of watering and should be mixed with composts in their dry state prior to potting or planting. Many hanging basket composts include these granules in their formulation.

Wattle Panels made from interwoven pliable twigs that were originally used by farmers to control their livestock. However, in a return to and appreciation of rural crafts they are now often used as decorative fence panels and screens in informal and cottage gardens. Being rough they provide ideal support for climbing and twining plants.

Weed This term refers to a plant that is growing in the wrong place which may go on to overcrowd its more desirable neighbours. The term is usually used to refer to a native plant that has arrived unexpectedly, but an invasive ornamental can be equally troublesome and be just as much a 'weed'.

Weedkiller A generic term used to describe chemicals that are applied to specific areas to kill weeds. Some are 'selective' in that they can be used to kill certain weeds only (such as those with broad leaves in a lawn).

Weeping A term used to describe the pendulous habit of certain plants. It may be a natural occurrence (willow, birch and larch), or the result of careful training and pruning (weeping standard roses).

Weevils A serious pest of ornamental plants, these are various species of beetle, most of which have a characteristically elongated snout. The larval stages are equally destructive causing serious damage to plant roots, bulbs, corms and tubers. The vine weevil is the most common and the larval stages can be controlled with insecticide drenches. Adults chew irregular holes in the leaves.

Adult pea and bean weevils eat their way right around the margins of the leaves while the larvae of the apple blossom weevil actually feed in the blossom bud, destroying it and drastically reducing the crop.

Wheelbarrow An essential piece of garden equipment for transporting heavy or bulky loads. Traditionally made of wood with a single wheel at the front and two handles behind, such barrows are now treated as more decorative than functional. Metals and plastics have taken over and even the traditional wheel has been replace in some models with a ball (ballbarrow) which is claimed to make the barrow easier to push and less damaging to lawns. Even the effort required to tip the barrow for loading and unloading can be avoided by choosing a model that is hinged on its frame.

Whip A term used to describe a grafted plant that has produced just one year's growth. At this stage the tree or shrub will have only one whip-like stem.

=maiden

Whip and tongue A type of graft where the stock and scion are prepared with complementary notches that increase the surface area available for union and also hold the two portions in place.

Whitefly Various tiny white winged insects that are particularly fond of greenhouse tomatoes and brassicas outside. Young growth is stunted by these sap-sucking insects.

In the confines of the greenhouse they can be controlled through the use of insecticide sprays or fumigations. Alternatively a biological control can be used (using the wasp *Encarsia formosa* which parasitizes the scale stage of the life cycle).

In the garden regular sprays with a suitable insecticide are effective.

White rot A soil-borne fungal disease that attacks onions, leeks, shallots and garlic. Leaves yellow, wilt and die as do the roots. Fluffy fungal growth may be seen on the bulbs. Chemical controls are available and infected ground should not be used for these crops for about five years.

White rust A fungal disease that causes dense white, felty outgrowths – most prevalent on brassicas, wallflowers and stocks. Suitable fungicides are available.

Whorl A term used to describe the circular arrangement of leaves or flowers around the node of a stem. The flowers of a candelabra primula are arranged in 'whorls'.

Widger A small forked hand tool designed for carefully lifting seedlings when pricking out. It catches the leaves between the forked prongs, so the young plant can be lifted without the delicate stem or roots having to be handled.

Wild garden A term used to describe a garden that is intended to re-create a piece of the countryside. It may seem like an excuse to sit back and do nothing letting nature take its course, but creating such a garden in an unnatural situation probably requires more skill and judgement than a 'conventional' garden.

Wildlife garden Although a vast number of animal and insect species are to be found in our gardens anyway, some gardeners like to combine one hobby with another – that of natural history. A careful selection of plants (usually native species) and the creation of varied habitats attracts a much greater range of wildlife.

Under such a regime the use of organic methods of pest and disease control should be observed and cultural methods may be adapted. A good example would be leaving wood and debris in part of the garden to provide cover and hibernation sites for animals and a plentiful supply of decaying organic matter for insects and fungi.

Wilt A disorder that may be brought about by physical means or disease where the leaves and young stems start to flag indicating that not enough water is reaching them.

Physical causes may be underwatering, overwatering (so the roots are deprived of oxygen and cannot function properly) or damage to the roots by a soil-borne pest.

Various fungal infections and viruses can cause similar symptoms and there are many that are specific to certain plants and named accordingly (such as aster wilt, clematis wilt).

Good garden hygiene and cultivation, chemical control and vigilance are all things that will help.

Wind The movement of air caused by areas of high and low pressure. The effect on plants and gardens can be marked, depending on the speed of such movement. In strong winds, plants (particularly trees) may be physically damaged or even torn from the ground, roots and all. More commonly the effect is to increase water lost from the plant through transpiration. This leads to wilting and ultimately a brown mottling of the foliage or leaf margins.

Plants will adapt and grow much more happily on the leeward side (away from the prevailing wind). The wind can create the spectacularly sculptured trees that can often be seen on quite exposed coastlines.

Window-box A container used to grow plants beneath a window. Almost as much of a national institution as the hanging basket, it enables a wide range of flowers to be grown in a limited space. Although requiring regular watering and feeding, window-boxes can also be used to grow certain fruits, vegetables and herbs.

Placed on the window-sill or supported on brackets beneath, a year-round display can be achieved by a bit of careful planning. Alternatively, successional plantings can be prepared in slightly smaller containers that can then be plunged into the window-box at the desired time.

Wind pollination The transfer of pollen from the anther (male) to the pistil (female) of a flower when the pollen is carried by the wind. Many trees use this method of fertilization, producing catkins that blow in the wind, distributing huge quantities of pollen into the breeze. The pollen of wind pollinated plants is fine and dust-like.

Windbreak A structure that protects from the wind. For the gardener this can be useful to protect early blossom from cold, frosty winds, and newly planted shrubs and conifers from the desiccating effect of winds. Effective windbreaks can be made from just about any material although special plastic webs and meshes are available to the amateur gardener. Being semi-permeable they filter the wind but still allow air and light to the protected plant.

When used to protect plants, the windbreak can be removed after a season so long as the plant is established.

Wing A membranous outgrowth from a seed or stem. In the case of some seeds (members of the acer family are a good example), the 'wing' helps to carry the seed on the wind ensuring greater distribution.

Winter gardens A term originally applied to large greenhouses and conservatories built by the Victorians so they could enjoy a 'garden' all year round. Often still found in fashionable seaside resorts and used for concerts and social events.

Nowadays the term is also used to describe gardens planted with trees, shrubs and perennials that provide a selection of winter interest – decorative stems, berries, etc.

Winter kill The result of damage from cold weather during the winter. Dead shoots and twigs should be pruned out in the spring. Some tender plants may be killed completely.

Winter moths A number of moths lay their eggs on fruit trees during the winter. The caterpillars hatch in early spring and set about devouring the young leaves, causing a severe check to the tree's natural growth. These are termed winter moths and include the mottled umber, winter moth and also the later laying March moth.

Females are wingless and hatch in the soil and then have to climb the tree to lay their eggs. The gardener can intercept this ritual by applying a band of grease around the tree to trap the ascending females. Alternatively, winter washes can be used to kill the eggs or insecticides to kill the caterpillars.

Winter pruning Pruning of deciduous trees carried out during the winter months while the tree is dormant and so will not be affected by such treatment. The harder the pruning, the more vigorous the new growth will be.

Winter wash A chemical control applied during the winter months to dormant fruit trees to kill overwintering insects, larvae, eggs and lichen.

Wireworms The worm-like larvae of some beetles that attack the roots of young plants and potato tubers. Slow moving and with three pairs of legs near their head end they may be confused with centipedes (although the latter are very active and have many more legs).

More of a problem on newly cultivated land (especially in the second year) they will be controlled by thorough and regular cultivation. Soil insecticides are also useful, as is trapping in slices of potato buried in the ground. These should be inspected every day and the wireworms destroyed.

Wireworms develop into smallish brown 'click' beetles – so named because of the strange noise they can make with their wings.

Witches' broom A natural phenomenon sometimes encountered in deciduous and evergreen trees and shrubs. Due to physical damage of the growing tissue (often by gall-forming insects), or as a result of fungal infection, shoots develop into a twisted, twiggy mass. They are often mistaken for birds' nests or squirrels' drays.

If the anomaly is due to a fungal infection, plants raised by vegetative means from the 'broom' will maintain the characteristics, and this is how many dwarf forms of conifer have been established.

Wood ash The ashes produced by a slow burning wood fire are naturally high in potash. This makes them a useful garden soil conditioner although the potash (in the form of carbonate of potash) is highly soluble and so the ash should be stored in a dry place if not required immediately.

Wood bud A bud that will develop into a shoot. The opposite of a fruit bud.

Woodland garden A garden created to recreate or enhance a lightly wooded site, using shade-loving shrubs, perennials, annuals and bulbs. The 'natural' garden has seen a revival in recent years – possibly as a result of gardeners wishing to escape their urban surroundings.

Woodlice Small armour-plated creatures, some species of which roll up into a ball when disturbed. This has earned them one of many common names – pillbugs. Black or greyish in colour they feed on decaying organic matter but can turn their attentions to young, soft-stemmed plants and ripening strawberries. Control can be achieved by practising good garden hygiene and trapping in scooped-out half potatoes placed on the soil. Chemical controls are also available.

Woody A stem that has become tough and fibrous.

Woolly aphid A species of aphid common on apple trees that covers itself with a protective cotton-wool-like substance. Attacking the wood, it causes swelling and cracks and some buds may be killed. Canker can be a secondary infection and can cause swollen bark and, in some cases, a thick sappy ooze. Insecticide sprays are effective but must be applied thoroughly to get into the bark crevices and a tar oil winter wash is a good preventative measure.

Worms The common earthworm is the gardener's friend, dragging dead leaves and other organic matter into the soil which increases the humus content. Their tunnelling activities aerate the soil and by ingesting soil they break it down into small particles enabling the quick release of plant nutrients.

The only place where earthworms are not welcome is on fine lawns of bowling green quality when this ingested soil is pushed to the surface in mounds or 'casts'. In mowing and rolling, these are flattened but they do lead to unevenness in the surface. Most gardeners are happy to brush off the worm casts with a besom broom before mowing the lawn although chemical worm killers are used in extreme circumstances.

X

Xenogamy Refers to the process of cross-fertilization.

Xerophyte A term used to describe a plant that has modified its structure so that it is capable of coping with a limited amount of water. Modifications may include the development of a thick, swollen stem that can be used as a reservoir, or the reduction of leaves and stems to limit the surface area available for transpiration. Cacti, succulents, heathers and brooms are good examples showing various degrees of modification.

Y

Yard Apart from the unit of imperial measurement equal to 0.9m, and an American term referring to a back garden, the term 'yard' is also used to refer to straight thin branches on a tree.

Yarfa A type of peat bog or peaty soil found in the Shetland Islands.

em Plant tissue through which water and olved nutrients are carried from roots to us parts of the plant. Also provides ¬anical support. Syn. **Wood**, Cf. **Phloem**.

Z

Zeatin A kinin.

Zinc This is a 'trace element' that is naturally occurring and required in minute amounts for plants to produce healthy growth.

Zygomorphic A term used to describe a flower structure that can be divided equally in two but only in one plane. A good example are individual flowers of a foxglove where the left hand side is a mirror image of the right (but the top half is totally different from the bottom half).

Hamlyn in association with **Amateur Gardening** also publish Stefan Buczacki's 'Best' series. A complete range of these titles, along with the handy Pocket Reference series, is available from all good bookshops or by Mail Order direct from the publisher. Payment can be made by credit card or cheque/postal orderin the following ways:

By Phone Phone through your order on our special CREDIT CARD HOTLINE on **0933 410511**. Speak to our customer service team during office hours (9am to 5pm) or leave a message on the answer machine, quoting your full credit card number plus expiry date and your full name and address. Please also quote the reference number shown at the top of this form.

By Post Simply fill out the order form below (it can be photocopied) and send it with your payment to: Reed Book Services Ltd, PO Box 5, Rushden, Northants NN10 6YX. **Special Offer**: Free Postage and Packaging for all orders over £10, add £2.00 for p+p if your order is for £10 or less.

ISBN	Title	Price	Quantity	Total
0 600 57698 1	Hellyer Pocket Guide	4.99		
0 600 57697 3	Gardener's Fact Finder	4.99		
0 600 58187 X	Dictionary of Plant Names	4.99		
0 600 58427 5	Pests, Diseases and Common Problems	4.99		
0 600 58428 3	Garden Terms	4.99		
0 600 57732 5	Best Climbers	4.99		
0 600 57735 X	Best Foliage Shrubs	4.99		
0 600 57734 1	Best Shade Plants	4.99		
0 600 57733 3	Best Soft Fruit	4.99		
0 600 58337 6	Best Water Plants	4.99		
0 600 58338 4	Best Herbs	4.99		
		Postage & Packaging (add £2 for p+p if your order is £10 or less)		
		GRAND TOTAL		

Name...(BLOCK CAPITALS)

Address...

....

....Postcode...............................

I enclose a cheque/postal order for £............made payable to Reed Book Services Ltd or

please debit my: Access [ ]   Visa [ ]   AmEx account [ ]   Diners [ ]

by £...............Expiry date...............Signature...............................

Account no [ ][ ][ ][ ][ ][ ][ ][ ][ ][ ][ ][ ][ ][ ][ ][ ]

Whilst every effort is made to keep our prices low, the publisher reserves the right to increase the prices at short notice. Your order will be dispatched within 28 days subject to availability.
Registered office: Michelin House, 81 Fulham Road, London SW3 6RB. Registered in England No 1974080
THIS FORM MAY BE PHOTOCOPIED